I0048217

UNLOCKING ISLAMIC CLIMATE FINANCE

NOVEMBER 2022

ASIAN DEVELOPMENT BANK

UNLOCKING ISLAMIC CLIMATE FINANCE

NOVEMBER 2022

ASIAN DEVELOPMENT BANK

Creative Commons Attribution 3.0 IGO license (CC BY 3.0 IGO)

© 2022 Asian Development Bank (ADB)
6 ADB Avenue, Mandaluyong City, 1550 Metro Manila, Philippines
Tel +63 2 8632 4444; Fax +63 2 8636 2444
www.adb.org

Some rights reserved. Published in 2022.

ISBN 978-92-9269-838-6 (print); 978-92-9269-839-3 (electronic); 978-92-9269-840-9 (ebook)
Publication Stock No. TCS220511-2
DOI: http://dx.doi.org/10.22617/TCS220511-2

The views expressed in this publication are those of the authors and do not necessarily reflect the views and policies of the Asian Development Bank (ADB) or its Board of Governors or the governments they represent.

ADB does not guarantee the accuracy of the data included in this publication and accepts no responsibility for any consequence of their use. The mention of specific companies or products of manufacturers does not imply that they are endorsed or recommended by ADB in preference to others of a similar nature that are not mentioned.

By making any designation of or reference to a particular territory or geographic area, or by using the term "country" in this document, ADB does not intend to make any judgments as to the legal or other status of any territory or area.

This work is available under the Creative Commons Attribution 3.0 IGO license (CC BY 3.0 IGO) https://creativecommons.org/licenses/by/3.0/igo/. By using the content of this publication, you agree to be bound by the terms of this license. For attribution, translations, adaptations, and permissions, please read the provisions and terms of use at https://www.adb.org/terms-use#openaccess.

This CC license does not apply to non-ADB copyright materials in this publication. If the material is attributed to another source, please contact the copyright owner or publisher of that source for permission to reproduce it. ADB cannot be held liable for any claims that arise as a result of your use of the material.

Please contact pubsmarketing@adb.org if you have questions or comments with respect to content, or if you wish to obtain copyright permission for your intended use that does not fall within these terms, or for permission to use the ADB logo.

Corrigenda to ADB publications may be found at http://www.adb.org/publications/corrigenda.

Notes:
ADB recognizes China as the People's Republic of China
In this publication, "$" refers to United States dollars.
In this publication, tables, figures, and maps without explicit sources are those of the authors.

Cover design by Ross Locsin Laccay

Photos: Steam from deep within the Earth is used to generate electricity at the Lahendong geothermal power plant in Manado, Indonesia; Women's group packaging coffee in Tunggul Bute village. The coffee production project is financed by Lahat, Geothermal Power Plan in South Sumatra, Indonesia. Phase I constitutes the geothermal resource exploration and drilling phase of project development; Sunny Bangchak solar farm in Chaiyabhum Province, Thailand; Water channel used to irrigate terraced farms in Nepal; Efficient transport is essential to achieve higher levels of economic growth needed for sustainable poverty reduction in Bangladesh; An agricultural field with the Burgos Wind Farm seen in the background; Suriya Athtar, 11, helping his family adopt safety measures to keep them safe during the COVID-19 lockdown in Pakistan; Construction workers wearing face masks while repairing a road in Phnom Penh, Cambodia; The City Government of Puerto Princesa, Philippines maintains nurseries of mangrove seedlings to complement the fisheries management project; Nine turbines in the turbine hall of the Nurek hydropower plant, Tajikistan; Bangladesh power plant; Hundreds of buses are parked at the Mohakhali bus terminal due to strike; Power lines and towers in Bhutan; Construction workers passing through the tunnels in Dagachhu hydropower Development in Bhutan. All photos by ADB.

Contents

Tables, Figures, and Boxes

TABLES

FIGURES

BOXES

Foreword

The magnitude of the climate crisis demands innovative ways to scale investment in climate action, including mobilizing new sources of climate finance. At the same time, the coronavirus disease (COVID-19) pandemic has added a new dimension to the climate crisis, reversing economic development gains, and further straining public resources to invest in climate action. Governments in Asia and the Pacific face a major challenge in defining the pathway for their economies to recover from this dual crisis.

This report assesses the potential of Islamic finance to support the climate agenda, and to help countries in the Asia and Pacific region deliver on their Paris Agreement goals. Islamic finance has thrived since its inception in the 1970s and is pegged at almost $3 trillion globally including in certain countries in Asia and the Pacific with significant Muslim populations. By examining the lessons and opportunities of implementing Islamic climate finance across countries in the region, the report proposes alternative pathways and implementation strategies to develop and implement Islamic finance for climate action and a green, resilient, and inclusive post–COVID-19 recovery.

The report recommends a staged approach, detailing four specific channels to target Islamic climate finance development: (i) greening Islamic capital markets, (ii) greening Islamic social finance, (iii) mobilizing Islamic project finance for green infrastructure and (iv) developing green banking services for the unbanked to support financial inclusion. This strategic approach aims to support countries in the region in a way that is tailored to their national context and the structure of their Islamic finance market.

The Asian Development Bank and the Islamic Development Bank share many common developing member countries in Asia and the Pacific, including those with high potential to scale up Islamic climate finance. We are therefore pleased to have collaborated on this study, combining our knowledge and perspectives on the challenges and opportunities of Islamic climate finance. We look forward to opportunities to work together to leverage the great potential of Islamic finance to support climate action and a green, inclusive, and resilient recovery from COVID-19.

WOOCHONG UM
Managing Director General,
OIC, Vice President Knowledge Management
and Sustainable Development
Asian Development Bank

DR. MANSUR MUHTAR
Vice President
Islamic Development Bank

Acknowledgments

This report was developed by the Asian Development Bank (ADB) in close collaboration with the Islamic Development Bank (IsDB).

The report was prepared by Salim Refas (consultant, ADB) under the guidance of Kate Hughes (senior climate change specialist, ADB), Esmyra Javier (climate change specialist, ADB), Ahmed Al Qabany (former manager, Climate Change Division, IsDB), and Daouda Ndiaye (lead climate change specialist, IsDB). Valuable inputs were also provided by Olatunji Yusuf (senior climate change specialist, IsDB), Bradley Hiller (lead climate change specialist, IsDB), Syed Husain Quadri (director, Resilience and Social Development Department, IsDB), Habib Abubakar (senior climate change specialist, IsDB), Zakky Bantan (manager, Capital Markets Division, IsDB), and Mohamed Hedi Mejaie (director, Investments Department, IsDB). The report was peer reviewed by staff from ADB including Arup Chatterjee (principal financial sector specialist), Mohd Sani Mohd Ismail (principal financial sector specialist) and Josh Ling (climate change specialist) and by Bradley Hiller and Olatunji Yusuf from IsDB.

The report benefited from inputs, insights and discussions with the list of persons mentioned in the Annex and the author would like to thank all experts interviewed for their valuable inputs.

The publication of this report was made possible by the valuable coordination and administrative support of Janet Arlene Amponin, Zarah Zafra, Anna Liza Cinco, and Maria Monica Edralin.

Abbreviations

AAOIFI	Accounting and Auditing Organization for Islamic Financial Institutions
ACGF	ASEAN Catalytic Green Finance Facility
ADB	Asian Development Bank
AIFC	Astana International Financial Centre
APIF	Awqaf Properties Investment Fund
ASEAN	Association of Southeast Asian Nations
AUM	asset under management
BAZNAS	Badan Amil Zakat Nasional (National Zakat Charity of Indonesia)
BCBS	Basel Committee on Banking Supervision
BNM	Bank Negara Malaysia
BREEAM	Building Research Establishment Environmental Assessment Method
CAF	Charities Aid Foundation
CCPT	Climate Change and Principle-based Taxonomy
DMC	developing member country
ESG	environmental, social, and governance
EU	European Union
GCC	Gulf Cooperation Council
GCF	Green Climate Fund
GDP	gross domestic product
GHG	greenhouse gas
GRI	Global Reporting Initiative
IBI	Islamic banking industry
ICF	Islamic climate finance
ICMA	International Capital Market Association
IFDI	Islamic Finance Development Indicator
IFI	international financial institution
IFSB	Islamic Financial Services Board
IFSI	Islamic financial services industry
IILM	International Islamic Liquidity Management
IMFI	Islamic microfinance institution
IPCC	Intergovernmental Panel on Climate Change
IPSF	International Platform on Sustainable Finance
IRI	Islamic Reporting Initiative
IsDB	Islamic Development Bank
ISF	Islamic social finance
KSA	Kingdom of Saudi Arabia
LEED	Leadership in Energy and Environmental Design

LLF	Lives and Livelihood Fund
MAF	Majid Al Futtaim
MDB	Multilateral development banks
MFI	Microfinance institutions
MIB	Maldives Islamic Bank
MSMEs	micro, small, and medium-sized enterprises
NBT	National Bank of Tajikistan
NDC	Nationally Determined Contributions
OCHA	Office for the Coordination of Humanitarian Aid
OECD	Organisation for Economic Co-operation and Development
OIC	Organization of Islamic Cooperation
OJK	Otoritas Jasa Keuangan (Indonesia Financial Services Authority)
PCG	Partial credit guarantees
PLS	Profit and loss sharing
PRB	Principles for Responsible Banking
PRC	People's Republic of China
PRI	Principles for Responsible Investment
RISE	Regional Infrastructure Supranational Entity
SDG	Sustainable Development Goal
SECO	Saudi Electricity Company
SME	small and medium-sized enterprises
SRI	sustainable and responsible investment
TA	technical assistance
TCFD	Task Force on Climate-Related Financial Disclosures
TSKB	Industrial Development Bank of Turkey
UAE	United Arab Emirates
UKIFC	United Kingdom Islamic Finance Council
UN	United Nations
UNDP	United Nations Development Programme
UNEP	United Nations Environment Programme
UNFCCC	United Nations Framework Convention on Climate Change
UNHCR	United Nations High Commissioner for Refugees
UNICEF	United Nations Children's Fund
UNRWA	United Nations Relief and Works Agency
US	United States
VBI	value-based intermediation
WACC	weighted average cost of capital

Executive Summary

In recent years across developing Asia, unexpected climate disasters have affected the lives and livelihoods of tens of millions of people. An even higher number of extreme climate disasters are expected to hit the region in upcoming years due to climate change and global warming. Since early 2020, the coronavirus disease (COVID-19) has severely hit the region and disrupted economies. To mitigate the combined effects of the climate crisis and COVID-19 pandemic, and to help economies adapt to expected future climate events, immediate and massive investments in low-carbon and climate-resilient infrastructure are urgently needed.

The Asian Development Bank (ADB) has committed to support its members in this effort. Under its Strategy 2030, the bank will increase the quantity of projects and overall investment toward climate change mitigation, climate and disaster resilience, and environmental sustainability. It will increase the quality of its interventions in mainstreaming of climate change mitigation, climate and disaster resilience, and environmental sustainability. ADB has committed to ensure that at least 75% of its operations focus on climate adaptation and mitigation efforts, while providing $100 billion in cumulative climate financing by 2030 to support these investment needs. Beyond its own resources, ADB is also committed to mobilizing additional financing and catalyzing alternative funding for the green, inclusive, and resilient economic recovery of its developing member countries (DMCs).

Islamic finance holds great potential to support post-COVID-19 recovery in ADB DMCs, and mobilize climate finance in line with the Paris agenda. Since its inception in the 1970s, the Islamic financial services industry (IFSI) has grown to an industry of almost $3 trillion globally. The industry is highly concentrated today in a few jurisdictions that have developed both the institutional infrastructure and the domestic demand for Islamic finance products and services. Among ADB members, Islamic finance is reported to attract a significant market share (more than 15%) of domestic banking sector assets in only four countries (Bangladesh, Brunei Darussalam, Malaysia, and Pakistan), and together with Indonesia, they concentrate today more than 98% of the $750 billion Islamic finance assets under management reported across ADB members.

The potential of Islamic finance to support a green, inclusive, and resilient post-COVID-19 recovery across the ADB members in common with the Islamic Development Bank (IsDB) has not been studied. This report addresses in part this research gap. Across Azerbaijan, Bangladesh, Brunei Darussalam, Indonesia, Kazakhstan, Kyrgyz Republic, Malaysia, Maldives, Pakistan, Tajikistan, Turkmenistan, and Uzbekistan ("common member countries"), the IFSI's level of development varies greatly. Their institutional and financial infrastructure for climate action in the context of the Paris Agreement are at various stages of maturity. The rapid and consistent growth of IFSI in Bangladesh, Indonesia, Malaysia, and Pakistan in the last 3 decades and its solid penetration in all finance sector segments contrasts markedly with the start-up stage of the industry in Central Asia, for example, where only a few Islamic banking and financial services offerings are reported. In this context, the development of IFSI is expected to remain differentiated across the common member countries in the next decade and highly concentrated in the leading IFSI markets. In parallel, a significant convergence with the global green finance agenda across common member countries is observed, both at the individual level, or at a subregional level through regional or multicountry initiatives.

The strategic importance of the climate change agenda for the Islamic finance industry has been recognized by the Islamic Declaration on Global Climate Change in 2015. The faith-based principles of Islamic finance support the protection of the environment, fair distribution of wealth, equal opportunities for all human beings, and avoidance of harm. As such, they provide a fundamental justification for a transition of the whole industry to a green and inclusive finance agenda. However, the principles fall short of practical application, and despite noticeable progress in environmental, social and governance (ESG) principles of the industry, leading Islamic finance thinkers and scholars have, in recent years, called for a change of paradigm for Islamic finance to support the achievement of the climate agenda and Sustainable Development Goals (SDGs). In parallel, leading IFSI institutions, whether multilateral agencies (e.g., IsDB), government agencies (e.g., Bank Negara Malaysia, BAZNAS) or private corporations (e.g., Maybank, CIMB, HSBC Amanah) have made considerable progress in adopting the climate action agenda and are leading the industry toward fast-paced mainstreaming of climate agenda and alignment with the Paris Agreement. The fundamental focus of Islamic finance on social impact, especially through Islamic social finance institutions (e.g., *Zakat* institutions, *Awqaf*), and the increased awareness of risks associated with climate change and climate disasters, provide another solid basis for supporting the green, inclusive and resilient recovery agenda among common member countries.

Multiple demand-side and supply-side obstacles prevent the rapid development of Islamic climate finance (ICF) across common member countries. For example, the principles of governance are still fragmented. Despite noticeable progress in recent years, governance standards of the industry are yet to be fully developed in line with global standards for climate action and Paris alignment. The development of common ESG or green taxonomies, and the development of human and institutional resources to mainstream green finance principles in operations are also required to support the transition of the industry. For Islamic capital market instruments specifically, implementation challenges include the absence of unified regulatory frameworks and legal documentation, the absence of unified accounting and reporting frameworks for climate or sustainability impacts, the high transaction costs for external review, and the difficult access to independent ratings of financial products during structuring stages due to low market maturity. On the demand-side, the availability of a sustained and growing pipeline of climate-related financing opportunities tailored to Islamic finance specific requirements, or shrinking public spending in climate finance as a consequence of COVID-19 economic and social impacts, are among the main factors preventing the growth of ICF.

Despite these challenges, the prospects of the industry are bright and multiple successes are reported in the adoption of the green finance agenda by IFSI players across common member countries in recent years. For example, the "ESG revolution" among various investor classes has pushed IFSI into a transformation pathway that supports a fast greening of the industry. In Malaysia, at least six ESG-themed funds have been launched in 2021 alone, while in 2020, only two such funds were introduced. Multiple *green sukuk* issuances, the flagship capital market product of Islamic finance, are reported in recent years with a mix of international issuances (e.g., Perusahaan Penerbit SBSN Indonesia III, IsDB) and domestic issuances in Malaysia, under the recently adopted Association of Southeast Asian Nations (ASEAN) Green Bonds standards. The increased awareness and appetite of investors has pushed the *sukuk* industry to rapidly progress in the rating of IFSI private debt securities by global (Fitch, Moody's and S&P) and regional (e.g., RAM Rating Agency Berhad in Malaysia) rating agencies, in the harmonization of the documentation to reduce implementation delays and address investor concerns and in the pricing of *sukuk* issuances, especially for mature issuers. Progress in the adoption of global reporting guidelines such as guidelines of the Task Force on Climate-Related Financial Disclosure has the potential to attract investors beyond traditional Islamic finance investors, therefore diversifying demand and growing the industry. High demand for Shari'ah-compliant consumer banking across unbanked populations of common member countries also holds one of the best potentials for the development of sustainable Islamic finance and ICF in the region. In Bangladesh, Kyrgyz Republic, Pakistan, and Tajikistan, in just 3 years between 2014 and 2017, the level of financial inclusion has increased by more than 50%. In Indonesia, the financial inclusion progressed by 35% over the same period. Yet, until today, more than half of the populations of Azerbaijan, Bangladesh, Indonesia, Kyrgyz Republic, Pakistan, or Tajikistan for example still do not own an account in a financial institution. This opens up great opportunities for the provision of Islamic banking services in line with the green, inclusive, and resilient recovery agenda. Beyond capital market products and consumer banking, two more segments of growth are expected to boost demand for climate finance in the Islamic finance industry: green infrastructure financing and Islamic social finance (ISF). In Indonesia alone, the potential of *zakat*, the obligatory charity, is estimated at $22 billion annually, i.e., roughly 22% of the total size of IFSI in the country. The ongoing greening of *zakat* programs (at least the programs of the central *zakat* authority BAZNAS) contributes significantly to the greening of the whole industry in the country. ISF programs focus particularly on the rights of future generations and intergenerational solidarity. As such, they are well-aligned with the objectives of a green, resilient, and inclusive future for all. In the context of climate disasters, the ISF sector has also demonstrated a formidable potential to raise funds for immediate response and for reconstruction efforts with climate-resilient infrastructure.

The development of ICF along the four main channels identified (greening Islamic capital markets, greening ISF, mobilizing Islamic project finance for green infrastructure and developing green banking services for the unbanked to support financial inclusion) will require targeted support programs and policies. A staged and tailored approach is also recommended to adapt to the level of maturity of the industry in each common member country. Looking at the prioritization of the initiatives, international green *sukuk* issuances, domestic green *sukuk* issuances but also green infrastructure funds and sustainable finance instruments appear as the most readily scalable Islamic finance instruments, especially in the developed Islamic finance markets such as Bangladesh, Indonesia, Malaysia and Pakistan, Other priorities are identified but require more attention on implementation challenges (e.g., in green social finance) or more attention on alignment with climate-finance principles (e.g., in ESG strategies and ESG theme funds). Given the high asset intensity of Islamic finance, and the concentration in specific sectors such as real estate and construction, developing ICF will require a strong focus of industry players in developing relevant products and financing modalities. Accordingly, there is a need to invest heavily into strategic research, support programs to accompany the main players in the industry into climate transition, and support the development of relevant products such as climate takaful or green *awqaf* or *zakat* programs.

The four channels proposed are complementary in their potential impact to support the mitigation, adaptation, and resilience agenda. For example, greening Islamic capital markets has so far mostly supported the climate change mitigation agenda with a majority of green *sukuk* directed toward renewable energy projects, particularly in Indonesia and Malaysia. On the other hand, greening ISF and providing Islamic banking services to the unbanked are two primary channels for climate adaptation and climate resilience of common member countries. The promotion of financial inclusion through the development of Islamic consumer finance across common member countries is essential for resilience to climate change and for tackling the disproportionate impacts of climate disasters on disadvantaged groups. Through targeting poor populations with no or low access to formal financial services, *zakat* or charity programs, for example, can help reduce the exposure of disadvantaged social groups to the impacts of climate change through targeted climate-smart investments (whether in communities or households) and at the same time address consequences of climate disasters through emergency support and humanitarian aid. *Awqaf* or Islamic microfinance also have a critical role to play to increase resilience of communities to climate change impacts and support adaptation of the local economies. Finally, targeted Islamic finance investments in climate-adapted infrastructure or agricultural programs in climate-vulnerable regions such as coastal lowland areas or arid and semi-arid regions can help address climate adaptation finance gaps.

Multilateral development banks, and ADB and IsDB in particular, are expected to play a key role in the development of ICF. They can provide catalytic financing in common member countries and beyond to mobilize the full potential of the sector to bridge climate investment gaps. For green *sukuk* to follow the growth path of green bonds (which boomed from $5 billion in 2010 to more than $270 billion 10 years later) a mature market infrastructure and a diverse and strong investor pool is required. ADB and IsDB can join forces with other multilateral agencies to develop a global Islamic climate fund, which would catalyze development of the niche industry, building upon recent successes in Indonesia, Malaysia or the Gulf countries. ADB and IsDB experience in jointly or separately establishing global funds and facilities with partner donors and agencies, and their AAA-rating and preferred creditor status, would be highly complementary to successful country experiences and programs to crowd-in global investors into ICF.

1 Introduction

Asia and the Pacific is one of the regions most vulnerable to climate change. The impacts of climate change are expected to be most acutely felt in developing countries. To mitigate the effects of the climate crisis and adapt the economies to expected future climate events, immediate and massive investments in low-carbon and climate-resilient infrastructure are urgently needed. In 2021 alone, 57 million people have been affected by unexpected climate disasters such as floods and cyclones in India, Indonesia, the People's Republic of China (PRC), the Philippines, and Thailand.[1] Substantial funding is required to support these populations to recover from disasters triggered by natural hazard and their corollary economic and social impacts. The emergence of the coronavirus disease (COVID-19) in early 2020 has added a new dimension to the climate crisis, reversing decades of economic development gains globally, and further straining public resources to invest in climate action. While the evolution of the pandemic is unclear after more than 2 years of waves of COVID-19 variants propagating swiftly across the globe and still more than 3 million daily cases in January 2022, governments in developing Asia are facing a major challenge in defining the pathway for their economies to recover from this dual crisis. In the summer 2022, Pakistan was devastated by one of the most dramatic flooding in human history causing a heavy toll of more than 1,200 lives, washing away infrastructure in entire regions and provoking the forced relocation of tens of millions of inhabitants.

Against this backdrop and in the context of a strengthening of the international commitments to further limit greenhouse gas (GHG) emissions, address climate change impacts, and adapt economies for a green, resilient and inclusive future, the developing member countries (DMCs) of the Asian Development Bank (ADB) face significant investment needs for climate change mitigation and adaptation. This is reflected in ADB Strategy 2030, which highlights the importance of tackling climate change, building climate and disaster resilience, and enhancing environmental sustainability under its operational priority 3 (OP3). The main focus of OP3 will be: (i) increasing the quantity of ADB projects and overall investment toward climate change mitigation, climate and disaster resilience, and environmental sustainability; and (ii) increasing the quality of ADB interventions with regard to mainstreaming of climate change mitigation, climate and disaster resilience, and environmental sustainability, integration across the water–food–energy security nexus, and overall delivery of the development impact and results. ADB has committed to ensure that at least 75% of its operations focus on climate adaptation and mitigation efforts, while providing $100 billion in cumulative climate financing by 2030 to support these investment needs. In addition, a key role for ADB and other multilateral development banks (MDBs) is to ensure that their capital resources are leveraged to mobilize additional financing, especially in the context of the COVID-19 pandemic, which has compounded issues faced by DMCs and put further pressure on raising public finance.

Islamic finance holds great potential to support a green, inclusive, and resilient post-COVID-19 recovery in ADB DMCs and to mobilize climate finance in line with the Paris agenda. This $3 trillion finance and investment industry globally has only marginally contributed to climate action to date. It has an estimated cumulative investments of only around $20 billion in climate finance, due to a range of demand and supply obstacles that can be addressed. The Islamic finance industry, although relatively marginal in the global financial architecture since its debut in the 1970s, is built upon ethical and responsible finance principles perceived to be much aligned with climate finance and sustainable finance principles. The transition of Islamic finance toward climate and sustainable finance principles is therefore a natural transition that can be catalyzed to mobilize assets

---

[1]   International Federation of Red Cross and Red Crescent Societies. https://www.ifrc.org/press-release/over-57-million-affected-climate-disasters-across-asia-pacific-2021 (accessed 27 January 2022).

of the industry for climate action and green, inclusive, and resilient recovery. The industry already offers a wide range of financial instruments that can support climate and recovery investments, in particular: capital market instruments such as green *sukuk*; social finance instruments such as green *awqaf*; restricted lines of finance in the banking sector (restricted *mudarabah*); or other financial products such as green Islamic funds, Islamic microfinance and *takaful*.

Conversely, a radical transition to climate finance and sustainable finance is a great opportunity for the Islamic finance industry to tap into a large and vastly untapped global investor base looking at sustainable and responsible investment options. The diversification of capital market investors into Islamic finance products observed in the last few years confirms the appetite of new investors in Islamic finance products when these products are structured as green or climate finance.

But as countries work toward achieving the climate targets pledged through their Nationally Determined Contributions (NDCs) under the Paris Agreement and other governmental commitments, the Islamic finance industry has not yet translated this potential into reality. This report is written in this context to analyze both opportunities and challenges to mobilize Islamic finance to support climate change actions and a green, inclusive, and resilient COVID-19 recovery in Asia and the Pacific.

2 Islamic Climate Finance: A Nascent Industry in a Double-Bind

2.1 Overview of the Islamic Finance Services Industry and Rationale for the Development of Islamic Climate Finance

Overview of the Islamic Finance Services Industry

Since its inception in the 1970s, **the Islamic financial services industry (IFSI) has grown to an industry of $2.88 trillion globally by end 2019. It is forecasted to grow to $3.69 trillion by end 2024.[2] This represents less than 1% of the global financial assets today.[3]** According to the Islamic Financial Services Board (IFSB),[4] the industry is highly concentrated into three geographical regions[5]: 42% of the global IFSI Asset Under Management (AUM) is concentrated in the Gulf Cooperation Council (GCC), as compared to 26% in the Middle East and South Asia excluding GCC, and 24% in Southeast Asia. In terms of market segments (Figure 1), Islamic Banking concentrates the majority of assets (72.4%), followed by *sukuk* (22.3%), funds (4.2%) and finally the nascent *takaful* market (1.1%).

Figure 1: Global Islamic Financial Services Industry Assets by Segment of the Industry
($ billion)

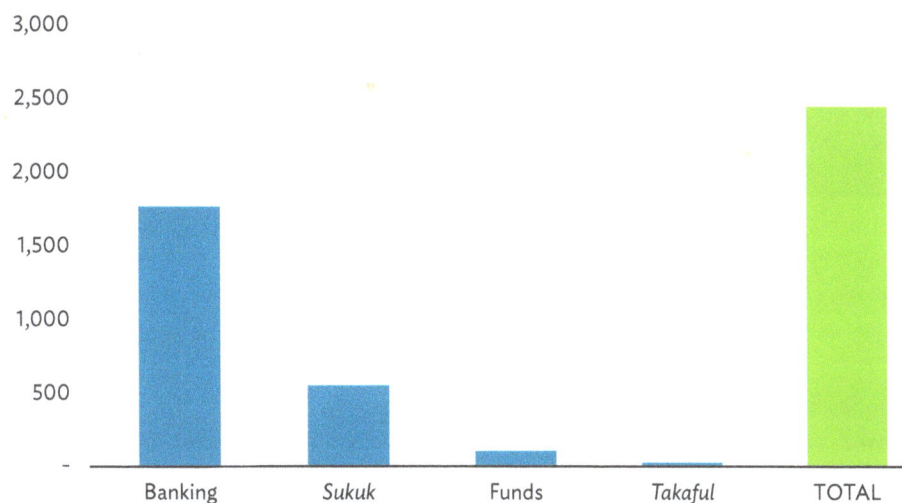

Source: Islamic Financial Services Board, Islamic Financial Services Industry Stability Report 2020.

---

[2]   ICD-Refinitiv. 2020. Islamic Finance Development Report. Jeddah, KSA. December.
[3]   Credit Suisse Research Institute. 2021. *Global Wealth Report*. Switzerland.
[4]   Due to different statistical resources, the IFSB reports a global IFSI AUM volume of $2.48 trillion by end 2019, i.e. a lower global volume than the volume of $2.88 trillion reported by ICD-Refinitiv (footnote 1).
[5]   IFSB. 2020. *Islamic Financial Services Industry Stability Report*. Kuala Lumpur, Malaysia. July.

As of 2019, according to the same sources (footnote 5), **91.4% of Islamic banking AUM are concentrated in the 13 jurisdictions where Islamic banking is of systemic importance,[6] and only three of them (Bangladesh, Brunei Darussalam and Malaysia) are among the Asian Development Bank (ADB) member countries.** In addition, the State Bank of Pakistan recently reported that Islamic banking has reached 18.7% market share in the overall banking industry, which would qualify Pakistan as a fourth ADB member country with an Islamic banking sector of systemic importance as of the end of 2020 (footnote 5).[7] Indonesia and the Maldives report a market share of the Islamic banking industry between 5% to 10% and the remaining ADB members have a penetration rate of Islamic banking in the overall banking sector below 2%.[8] Despite its significance in four countries in the region, the IFSI sector is **still a marginal finance sector in Asia,** even in countries with majority Muslim populations (Table 1).

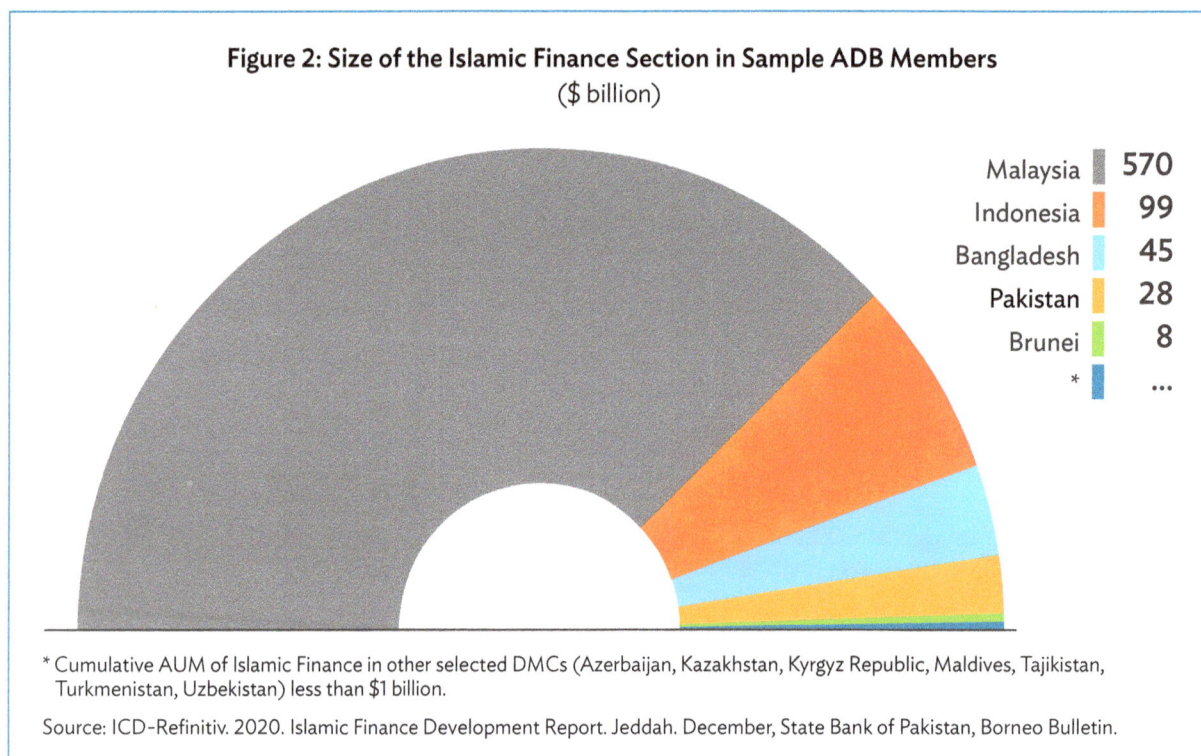

Figure 2: Size of the Islamic Finance Section in Sample ADB Members
($ billion)

Malaysia	570
Indonesia	99
Bangladesh	45
Pakistan	28
Brunei	8
*	...

* Cumulative AUM of Islamic Finance in other selected DMCs (Azerbaijan, Kazakhstan, Kyrgyz Republic, Maldives, Tajikistan, Turkmenistan, Uzbekistan) less than $1 billion.

Source: ICD-Refinitiv. 2020. Islamic Finance Development Report. Jeddah. December, State Bank of Pakistan, Borneo Bulletin.

According to the lastest issue of the Islamic Finance Development Report by ICD-Refinitiv (footnote 2), **the two countries with the most developed Islamic finance sectors in the world are Malaysia and Indonesia respectively.** The Islamic banking industry has more assets under management in Iran and Saudi Arabia (footnote 5). However, Malaysia and Indonesia demonstrate a stronger performance in the production of knowledge in Islamic finance, in the awareness of IFSI products and regulations, and in the development of governance of the sector. These reinforce their global position as leaders in the industry. In 2020, Malaysia remains the global leader in the global Islamic Finance Development Indicator (IFDI) of ICD-Refinitiv while Indonesia has jumped in the latest ranking from fourth position globally to the second position. At the same time, the biggest increase in quantitative development indicators for the IFDI 2020 were recorded by the Central Asian nations of Tajikistan and Uzbekistan after they each introduced Islamic banking, which underscores the strong potential of the nascent IFSI sectors in other Asian countries.

---

[6] According to IFSB, countries classified having a more than 15% share of Islamic banking assets in their total domestic banking sector asset
[7] State Bank of Pakistan. 2021. *Islamic Banking Bulletin*. Karachi, Pakistan. March
[8] See Appendix 1 for a brief review of Islamic banking sector in ADB DMCs.

Figure 3: Growth of the Islamic Financial Services Industry Assets under Management in 2013–2020 in Sample ADB Developing Member Countries
($ billion)

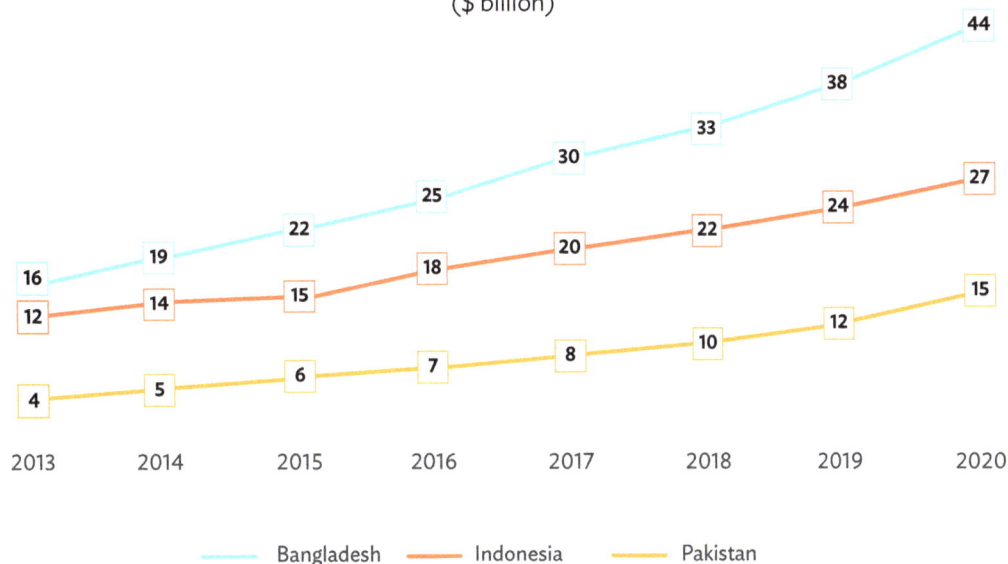

Source: Prudential and Structural Islamic Financial Indicators (PSIFIs) for Islamic Banks (accessed 22 August 2021) https://www.ifsb.org/psifi_03.php#.

ADB has 14 DMCs with a majority Muslim population, five of which are among the 10 countries with the largest Muslim populations in the world.[9] ADB has 13 member countries[10] in common with the Islamic Development Bank (IsDB) and are the main scope of this report: Azerbaijan, Bangladesh, Brunei Darussalam, Indonesia, Kazakhstan, Kyrgyz Republic, Malaysia, Maldives, Pakistan, Tajikistan, Turkmenistan, and Uzbekistan ("common member countries").[11]

In these countries, IFSI shows a large growth potential and has been identified by ADB[12] as "an alternative financing source for infrastructure and economic development in Asia," as well as "a source of investment financing in both advanced and emerging economies," and "a means for diversifying funding and broadening risk exposures at both institutional and macroeconomic levels." Yet, challenges related to capacity of supervisory authorities and market players, as well as the legal and regulatory frameworks, have impeded the development of the industry. ADB has recently undertaken and contributed to several initiatives to overcome such challenges. ADB has recently undertaken and contributed to several initiatives to overcome such challenges in the common member countries and beyond. An example of such initiatives is the ongoing knowledge and support technical assistance (TA) in the Philippines to develop a regulatory framework appropriate for sustainable Islamic finance operations and capacity building activities for selected regulators in the country.[13]

[9]   ADB. Finance sector. https://www.adb.org/what-we-do/sectors/finance/islamic-finance.
[10] Common member country includes Afghanistan, however, ADB placed on hold its assistance in Afghanistan effective 15 August 2021. ADB Statement on Afghanistan | Asian Development Bank (published on 10 November 2021). Manila. This report was prepared based on the information available for Afghanistan as of 31 July 2021.
[11] Data retrieved on 22 August 2021 at https://www.pewforum.org/chart/interactive-data-table-world-muslim-population-by-country/.
[12] ADB. 2015. Islamic Finance for Asia: Development, Prospects, and Inclusive Growth. Manila. May.
[13] ADB. Philippines: Islamic Finance for the Philippines. Project No. 50325-001. https://www.adb.org/projects/50325-001/main.

From a structural point of view, a fundamental challenge faced by central banks, financial institutions, and development agencies, including ADB, is that IFSI is different from conventional finance. It typically involves real economy transactions such as sale and purchase agreements and partnership investment structures, which need to be structured differently from typical banking products in conventional finance. The prohibition of interest in Islamic finance is a major challenge to these institutions, which typically finance operations through the issuance of conventional interest-bearing bonds or borrowing in private markets or through private placements. IFSI has therefore initially developed independently from conventional finance and despite solid two-digit growth rates, its share in global finance volumes has remained limited. Even in the case of conventional finance institutions developing "Islamic windows," principles of prudence have required among others the segregation of funds and resulted in the establishment of different capital funds, accounts, and reporting systems for conventional and Islamic finance activities.[14] Yet, with the growing recognition that many Islamic finance products eventually "replicate the economic effect of conventional products"[15] and share similar characteristics driven by demand for financing and investment products, Islamic banking has been "steadily moving into an increasing number of conventional financial systems" in the last 3 decades, has implemented conventional reporting systems (in particular International Financial Reporting Standards [IFRS]), has developed a wide range of products to match demand from Muslim and non-Muslim customers, and eventually has made its way in the global financial markets (footnote 14).

Table 1: Asian Countries with the Largest Estimated Muslim Population (million)

Country	Estimated Muslim population
Indonesia*	202,87
Pakistan*	174,08
India	160,95
Bangladesh*	145,31
Afghanistan* / **	28,07
Uzbekistan*	26,47
People's Republic of China	21,67
Malaysia*	16,58
Kazakhstan*	8,82
Azerbaijan*	8,68

* Common member country of Asian Development Bank and Islamic Development Bank. See footnote 16.
** See footnote 10.

See Appendix 1 for a brief review of Islamic banking sector in common member countries.

According to the Pew Research Center database on World Muslim Population by Country, ADB DMCs are home to 62% of the global Muslim population, with 45% of the global Muslim population located in Indonesia, Pakistan, India, and Bangladesh alone.[16] Despite obstacles to the development of IFSI (discussed in part in section 1.2), the growth of the industry has been consistent since the 1990s. **But this growth performance is markedly different across geographies and the industry is growing in developing Asia in a two-tiered pattern: a rapid and consistent growth of IFSI in three DMCs (Bangladesh, Indonesia, and Pakistan), which is now significant compared to the conventional finance sector, and the birth of a new financial industry in other DMCs, which**

---

[14]　Sole, J. A. 2007. Introducing Islamic Banks into Coventional Banking Systems. *International Monetary Fund Working Paper*. Washington, DC.
[15]　Malaysian Accounting Standards Board. 2012. A Word about Islamic Finance.
[16]　Pew Research Center. Interactive Data Table: World Muslim Population by Country (accessed 22 August 2021) https://www.pewforum.org/chart/interactive-data-table-world-muslim-population-by-country/

has not reached significance despite its potential. The significant progress in institutional infrastructure for IFSI in Central Asia or East Asia in recent years (footnote 2), and the potential penetration due to demographics of the Muslim population in these regions, has not yet converted into a significant penetration of Islamic banking and financial services. This development is likely to be staged according to supply and demand-side obstacles. The industry has grown in recent years beyond its traditional markets of countries that are members of the Organization of Islamic Cooperation (OIC), and multiple Islamic financial institutions operate in other ADB DMCs such as Sri Lanka, Thailand, or the Philippines, although with relatively marginal customer bases at this stage.[17]

The Islamic finance industry is entering its fifth decade of existence in the modern era but its development path in the post-COVID context is uncertain. The internationalization of IFSI from the traditional markets in GCC and Malaysia has been fueled by two major drivers: (i) the improvements in the Islamic finance architecture orchestrated by the setup of global regulatory agencies and standard-setting institutions, which have contributed to quickly setting up regulations and standards for Islamic finance in new markets (including in non-OIC countries such as the United Kingdom or Singapore), and (ii) the internationalization of major IFSI players—in particular, GCC banks, which opened channels or partner institutions in new countries. For example, Dubai Islamic Bank, the second largest Islamic bank by total assets in 2020[18] has expanded during its 4 decades of history to Bosnia, Jordan, Pakistan, Sudan and Türkiye, often playing a key role in developing IFSI in these markets, and it is still expanding to new geographies in Asia and Africa.[19]

Similarly, Kuwait Finance House, the third largest IFSI banking group, has been instrumental in developing IFSI in Türkiye, through the creation of the Kuveyt Turk participation bank, which is now the largest participation bank in the country. Al Baraka Group, the ninth largest Islamic bank by total assets in 2020, is also one of the most international Islamic bank with presence in 17 countries and has contributed to developing the industry in multiple markets in Arab and Asian countries.[20] In the context of global and economic financial crisis, the dominant trend is expected to be a consolidation of global presence to mature markets rather than aggressive development strategies in frontier markets.[21] Accordingly, this could put a halt to the development of IFSI in countries where the industry has not yet reached systemic importance.

At the same time, Islamic finance has developed in mature markets including in Asia, Europe, and the United States as a means of diversifying funding and risk exposures of conventional investors[22] and serving as a source of stability of the global financial system against factors such as overleverage and short-termism.[23] In the wake of the 2008 global financial crisis, Islamic institutions garnered some attention for faring better than their conventional counterparts but in the post-COVID-19 context, due to higher exposure of the Islamic banking industry to small and medium-sized enterprises (SMEs) and retail lending, the performance of the sector is uncertain.[24]

---

[17] This report is mainly focused on the common member countries of the ADB and IsDB and therefore limited reference will be made in the following sections on the countries non-member of the OIC.
[18] The Asian Banker. The Largest Banks Rankings. https://www.theasianbanker.com/ab500/2018-2019/largest-islamic-banks (accessed 10 July 2021).
[19] *World Finance*. 2014. Dubai Islamic Bank eyes strong global presence. Interview with Dr Adnan Chilwan, CEO, Dubai Islamic Bank. 14 March. https://www.worldfinance.com/banking/dubai-islamic-bank-eyes-strong-global-presence accessed on 07/10/2021.
[20] alBaraqa. Global Network. 2021. https://www.albaraka.com/en/about-al-baraka/about-us/global-network (accessed on 10 July 2021).
[21] Interviews with senior IFSI executives from the GCC region (July 2021).
[22] Islamic Development Bank Group and World Bank, 2018. Global Report on Islamic Finance: The Role of Islamic Finance in Financing Long-term Investments. *Overview booklet*. Washington, DC: World Bank and IsDBG. License: Creative Commons Attribution CC BY 3.0 IGO.
[23] Komijani, A. and F. Taghizadeh-Hesary. 2018. An Overview of Islamic Banking and Finance in Asia. *ADBI Working Paper 853*. Tokyo: Asian Development Bank Institute.https://www.adb.org/publications/overview-islamic-banking-and-finance-asia.
[24] Oxford Business Group. 2020. After Covid-19, what is next for Islamic banking? https://oxfordbusinessgroup.com/news/after-covid-19-what-next-islamic-banking (accessed on 10 October 2021).

In traditional Islamic economics literature, human beings are perceived as an integrated unit, exerting their economic behavior within the boundaries of a moral screening.[25] In particular, the moral accountability of every human being for all their actions is fundamental, even in the context of financial intermediation and the individual responsibility of any economic agent to inquire about the impacts of their economic decisions is not "excused" or transferred in the exercise of investment decisions.

Another principle, which underpins the rationale for climate action in the context of Islamic economics and finance, lies in the principle of "vicegerency," whereby human beings as "inheritors" of the earth, have a moral duty to preserve it and protect it, for future generations and simply as a trusted deposit.[26]

Box 1. What is Islamic Finance?

Islamic Finance is a set of faith-based financial intermediation products and institutions, asset-backed, promoting ethical, sustainable, and environmentally and socially responsible finance for all. It promotes risk sharing, connects the finance sector with the real economy, and emphasizes financial inclusion and social welfare.[a] It prohibits interest, gambling, speculation, uncertainty and imposes dealing exclusively with Shari'ah legitimate assets within existence and with proper ownership. The ethical principles guiding Islamic Finance are faith-based and imply the superposition of a moral and Shari'ah screening of any transaction, but they converge in practice with the main principles of responsible finance. Islamic Finance has historically developed from a set of classical finance contracts practiced throughout Islamic history, but the recent decades have seen the booming of the industry on the basis of hybrid contracts fitting modern needs for financial intermediation.[b]

---

[a]   World Bank 2015. Islamic Finance. https://www.worldbank.org/en/topic/financialsector/brief/islamic-finance.
[b]   Asian Development Bank.

Islamic economics fully recognize principles of economic freedom and equitable access to economic opportunities, which are common with conventional economic systems. The principles of private and public ownership are also respected and guaranteed, with another form of ownership, *awqaf* properties, a social finance instrument specific to Islamic economic systems. Here, the ownership of a productive asset is held permanently or for a specified period of time in a specific legal setup, wherein the property cannot be disposed-off while its income and usufruct are dedicated to a specified cause or beneficiaries.[27]

Finally, the strong principles of justice imply the prohibition of any aggression against rights and properties of others. By the same principles, the rights and properties of future generations are to be respected and preserved by current generation.

The strategic importance of the climate change agenda for the Islamic finance industry has been recognized by the Islamic Declaration on Global Climate Change in 2015.[28] Faith leaders, international development policy makers, academics, and other representatives called on governments prior to the Paris Agreement to "bring their discussions to an equitable and binding conclusion" bearing in mind: "(i) the scientific consensus on climate change,

---

[25]   Asutay, M. 2013. *Islamic moral economy as the foundation of Islamic finance. In Islamic Finance in Europe.* Edward Elgar Publishing.
[26]   Haqqi, A. R. 2014. Shariah governance in Islamic financial institution: An appraisal. US-China L. Rev. Vol. 11, p. 112.
[27]   Kahf, M. 2003. *The role of waqf in improving the ummah welfare.* Paper presented at the International Seminar on Waqf as a Private Legal Body organized by the Islamic University of North Sumatra Medan, Indonesia, pp. 6–7.
[28]   https://unfccc.int/news/islamic-declaration-on-climate-change.

which is to stabilize greenhouse gas concentration in the atmosphere at a level that would prevent dangerous anthropogenic interference with the climate systems; (ii) the need to set clear targets and monitoring systems; (iii) the dire consequences to planet Earth if we do not do so; and (iv) the enormous responsibility the Conference of Parties shoulders on behalf of the rest of humanity, including leading the rest of us to a new way of relating to God's Earth."[29]

The declaration provides an important overarching framework for Islamic-compliant climate action.

Figure 4: Main Principles of Islamic Economics Underpinning Islamic Climate Finance

JUSTICE
no harm to other human beings, to the fauna and flora and to future generations
COMPASSION
moral standards of the Islamic institutions of charity and solidarity
EQUITY
equal opportunities for all, including women and vulnerable groups
Islamic Climate Finance
VICEGERENCY
moral duty to preserve the trusted deposits of Earth fauna and flora
FAIRNESS
public ownership and equitable use of "commons"
ACCOUNTABILITY
for economic decisions and harm caused to others

Source: Asian Development Bank.

Importance of Environmental Considerations in Islamic Economics

The principles of Islamic finance support the protection of the environment, fair distribution of wealth, equal opportunities for all human beings, and avoidance of harm. In the literature, Dien (1997)[30] is one of the earliest attempts to address the relationship between Islam and ecology through an application to water distribution

[29] United Nations. 2015. Islamic Declaration on Climate Change. https://unfccc.int/news/islamic-declaration-on-climate-change.

[30] Dien, M. I. 1997. Islam and the environment: Theory and practice. *Journal of Beliefs and Values*, 18(1): pp. 47–57.

specifically. Meanwhile, Foltz (2003)[31] is a more comprehensive attempt to address the Islamic perspective on ecology and rightly identifies cultural and societal obstacles, which until today, pose an obstacle to the development of an environmental ethic in Muslim countries. Islam (2004)[32] adopts a more fundamental perspective on the Islamic view of a "green Earth" defined as a "gift of God Almighty" to humans, which must be preserved at the individual, collective, national and global levels. In such normative discourse, the religious justifications for the preservation of the environment are very solid.

But **these approaches generally fall short of practical application** in the Islamic finance industry or Islamic economy today despite the growing levels of awareness of climate change and climate risks for current and future generations. Criticizing the low level of development thinking within scholars of Islamic jurisprudence, Ramadan (2009)[33] argues that climate change is among the challenges that would require a complete new approach of Islamic ethics,[34] whereby renewed higher objectives of the Shari'ah (*Maqasid al Shari'ah*) should explicitly include the higher objective of the preservation of the environment. Theoretically, this would imply that no Shari'ah screening would allow for investments in economic activities harmful to the environment.

Meanwhile, other calls for reforms, such as the call for paradigm change by Khan (2019),[35] identify the need for reform not at the level of Shari'ah governance but rather at the level of economic planning and decision-making. Khan argues that the ethical foundations of Islam already embed higher level principles that would support a **modified paradigm for Islamic finance and economy to support achievement of the Sustainable Development Goals (SDGs) and a transition to a circular economy.** The onus would be on a good understanding of core principles such as the rights of future generations, and an integration of the moral standards of the "institutions of compassion" as the author calls them (*awqaf, zakat, qard* and forbearance) into mainstream economic activities to drag the whole economy into more ethical activities preserving the nature and the environment. Compliance to strict environmental standards under this framework could be imposed on various levels such as during the Shari'ah screening of investments and financing and at the level of feasibility study or during implementation stages.

Importance of Social Considerations in Islamic Economics

While the climate and environmental considerations in IFSI investment decisions requires a paradigm change [36]and regulatory reforms, the social considerations have always been central in Islamic finance. Islamic finance is established on the premises that the well-being (falah) of all humans is achievable as long as fundamental principles of the Shari'ah such as justice, equity, fairness, or compassion are imposed and respected.[37]

---

31 Foltz, R. 2003. *Islam and ecology: a bestowed trust.* Center for the Study of World Religions, Harvard Divinity School.
32 Islam, M. M. 2004. Towards a green earth: an Islamic perspective. *Asian Affairs,* 26(4):pp. 44–89.
33 Ramadan, T. 2009. *Radical Reform: Islamic Ethics and Liberation.* Oxford University Press.
34 Ramadan suggests among others a new geography of the sources of *Usûl al-fiqh* (principles of jurisprudence), which would lead to integrating the Universe and social and human environments (and therefore all related sciences) into the formulation of the ethical finalities of Islam's message. This way, preservation of the environment would specifically integrate the higher ethical finalities of Islam and become not a means to achieve the other higher objectives of the Shari'ah, but a higher objective in itself.
35 Khan, T. 2019. Reforming Islamic finance for achieving sustainable development goals. *Journal of King Abdulaziz University: Islamic Economics,* 32(1).
36 While it is important to note that leading Islamic banking and finance scholars are dominantly of the opinion that a paradigm change is needed to mainstream responsible, sustainable climate finance in IFSI (footnote 35, interviews with IFSI executives July 2021), the extent and nature of this paradigm change is not consensual. The discussion of these various opinions is beyond the scope of this paper but these include the transition to a value-based intermediation model as advocated in particular by Bank Negara Malaysia (BNM) since 2018, the introduction of positive screening of Islamic finance transactions (e.g., Sadiq, R., & Mushtaq, A. 2015. The role of Islamic finance in sustainable development. *Journal of Islamic Thought and Civilization.* 5(1: pp. 46-65), the adoption of international principles of responsible finance and ESG governance tools (e.g., Sairally, B. S. 2015. Integrating environmental, social and governance factors in islamic finance: Towards the realisation of *maqasid al-shari'ah. ISRA International Journal of Islamic Finance,*7: p. 145), the institutionalization of Islamic social banking to overcome the social (and ecological) failure of IFSI (Asutay, M. 2007. Conceptualisation of the second best solution in overcoming the social failure of Islamic finance: Examining the overpowering of homoislamicus by homoeconomicus. *IIUM Journal in Economics and Management,* 15: pp. 67–195), or the full transition of Islamic finance to the circular economy principles (e.g., footnote 35, Hassan, M. K., Saraç, M., and Alam, A. W. 2020. Circular economy, Sustainable development, and the role of Islamic finance. *Islamic Perspective for Sustainable Financial System.* Istanbul: Istanbul University Press. pp. 1–26).
37 Chapra, M. U. 1993. Islam and economic development. Islamabad. Islamic Research Institute.

The instruments of Islamic social finance (ISF),[38] in particular the redistributive *zakat* system, the voluntary donations (*sadaqah*), the perennial *awqaf* endowments, the Islamic microcredit institutions or the cooperative insurance systems of takaful, are designed to support the most vulnerable populations without impeding the economic development of individuals and nations. Their potential contribution to the modern social agendas is substantial. For example, the United Nations Development Programme (UNDP) estimates that *zakat* alone could help mobilize $200 billion to $1 trillion annually for the SDGs agenda.[39]

Rationale for the Development of Islamic Climate Finance in the Context of Post-COVID-19 Recovery and the Climate Change Agenda

The first conclusions of the Sixth Assessment Cycle of the Intergovernmental Panel on Climate Change (IPCC)[40] have reinforced the conclusions of global climate experts: "emissions of greenhouse gases from human activities are responsible for approximately 1.1°C of warming since 1850-1900, and (...) averaged over the next 20 years, global temperature is expected to reach or exceed 1.5°C of warming." In Asia specifically, IPCC predicts with high confidence increasing heat extremes and decreasing cold extremes, increasing marine heatwaves, increasing average and heavy precipitations, decreasing surface wind speeds and lengthening and intensifying fire weather seasons, declining glaciers, and permafrost or glacial mass areas, and rising regional sea levels.

These climate risks have also been reported in ADB Country Climate Risk studies (Table 2) and the **rapid onset and long-term changes in key climate parameters for ADB DMCs highlight dramatic climate vulnerabilities in the 21st century that require immediate and massive investments in low-carbon and climate-resilient infrastructure, as well as substantial climate recovery needs.**

These investment gaps are even more acute in the context of post-COVID-19 recovery, which has caused further strains on public finances for DMCs. The alternative financing sources that can be potentially mobilized through IFSI to meet these infrastructure and economic development needs are of increasing importance.

Table 2: Summary Climate Vulnerabilities and Projections of Temperature Warming in Sample ADB Developing Member Countries Common with the Islamic Development Bank

AZERBAIJAN	KYRGYZ REPUBLIC	INDONESIA	PAKISTAN	TURKMENISTAN
• Up to +4.7°C by 2090	• Up to +5.3°C by 2090	• Up to +1.4°C by 2050	• Up to +4.9°C by 2090	• Up to +5.1°C by 2090
• Higher desertification and soil salinity	• Heat stress in lowland regions	• High exposure to flooding and extreme heat	• Changes to rainfall and runoff regimes causing yield declines	• Severe water shortages
• Reduction in agricultural productivity	• Drought incidence and expanded arid land	• High exposure to sea-level rise and permanent flooding	• Extreme river and coastal flooding	• Increase in drought frequency
• Health and Poverty issues	• Flooding and landslide hazards	• Multiple threats to food security	• Heat-related sicknesses and deaths for urban dwellers and outdoor laborers	• Food shortages and higher poverty incidence

Source: ADB. 2021. Climate Risk Country Profiles. Manila. June.

---

38 Otherwise referred to as institutions of compassion in the Islamic economic system (footnote 35).
39 Noor, Z., & Pickup, F. 2017. The role of *Zakat* in supporting the sustainable development goals. *UNDP Brief.* New York: UNDP.
40 IPCC. 2021 Sixth Assessment Report, Work Group 1, *Climate Change 2021: The Physical Science Basis.* Geneva-Switzerland, August. https://www.ipcc.ch/report/sixth-assessment-report-cycle/.

Despite the growing awareness of the important role of IFSI to support the climate agenda and help bridge climate investment gaps, and despite the widespread adoption of the SDGs agenda and the Paris Agreement by DMCs, it was not until the late 2000s that the theme of environmental sustainability emerged in the specialized literature and the IFSI industry. **ICF is still a niche market in IFSI.** According to estimates, **the ICF industry accounts for less than 2% of the IFSI industry today** and despite positive recognition of the importance of accelerating the transition to low-carbon development pathways, the industry needs strong support to rapidly transition to climate-resilient and climate-friendly development pathways.

The increasing recognition of climate risks across IFSI markets and the growing understanding of the catastrophic economic and social consequences of expected climate disasters in the next decades have awoken the IFSI stakeholders to the urgency of the challenge. It is reported for example, that during 1992–2011, Bangladesh, Djibouti, Guyana, and Tajikistan have each lost on average at least 2% of their gross domestic product (GDP) due to extreme weather events.[41] **The leading institutions** (e.g., IsDB[42]) **in IFSI have started to adopt both the SDGs and the Paris Agreement agenda in their corporate strategies, and at the same time an increasing number of regulatory bodies are working on sustainability standards or climate standards for the industry.**

In its 2020–2025 Climate Action Plan, the IsDB identifies the following priorities to accelerate the transition of its member countries to more resilient and sustainable economies and to align its operations with the global climate agenda: "(i) increased capacity within the Bank and among key stakeholders in member countries; (ii) a sustained and growing pipeline of climate-related financing opportunities; (iii) a sustained ability to mobilize additional resources and access to concessional sources of funding (including climate finance); and (iv) increased requests from member countries for these services".[43] Through this 2020–2025 Climate Action Plan, as a pioneer in IFSI, the IsDB has pledged to a climate finance target of 35% of total financial commitment by 2025. The Climate Action Plan will be implemented in line with the MDB Paris Alignment Framework, developed and agreed upon in 2017.[44] It has also set out modalities for achieving IsDB's climate finance target of 35% by 2025 and has been instrumental in mainstreaming climate action in the IsDB core sector policies and related operational strategies, including agriculture and rural development, energy, transport, health, urban development and water policies. In Malaysia, Maybank (the largest Islamic bank through its Islamic banking arm Maybank Islamic) committed in May 2021 to a carbon-neutral position of its emissions by 2030 and to achieving an operational net-zero carbon emissions by 2050. Through the Collective Commitment to Climate Action (CCCA), CIMB Islamic has also committed to align its portfolio in line with the Paris Agreement temperature targets and to "help facilitate the economic transition necessary to achieve climate neutrality".[45] Yet, as will be discussed in the next sections, the challenges to scale up ICF are many, and multiple pathways can be proposed.

2.2 Identifying Challenges to the Scale-up of Islamic Climate Finance

Intra-Industry Obstacles Preventing the Rapid Scale-Up of Islamic Climate Finance

Among the main obstacles to the rapid development of Islamic climate finance (ICF), the principles of governance arise as one of the first challenges.[46] The governance framework of the global IFSI has taken time to develop and until today the industry is fragmented between different regulatory environments as summarized in Figure 5.

---

[41] Sillah, B. 2017. Economic Impacts of Climate Change: Evidence from OIC Member Countries. *Journal of Economics and Development Studies*, 5(4): pp. 71–78.

[42] IsDB. 2019. *The Road to the SDGs, The President's Programme: A New Business Model for a Fast-Changing World.* Jeddah-KSA.

[43] IsDB. 2020. *The 2020-2025 Climate Action Plan.* Jeddah-KSA.

[44] The MDB Paris Alignment Framework was jointly developed by The African Development Bank Group, the Asian Development Bank, the Asian Infrastructure Investment Bank, the European Bank for Reconstruction and Development, the European Investment Bank, the Inter-American Development Bank Group, the Islamic Development Bank, the New Development Bank, and the World Bank Group (International Finance Corporation, Multilateral Investment Guarantee Agency, World Bank).

[45] Collective Commitment to Climate Action, UNEP Finance Initiative.

[46] Interview with Islamic finance experts, July 2021.

Figure 5: Building Blocks of the Governance Framework of the Islamic Finance Industry

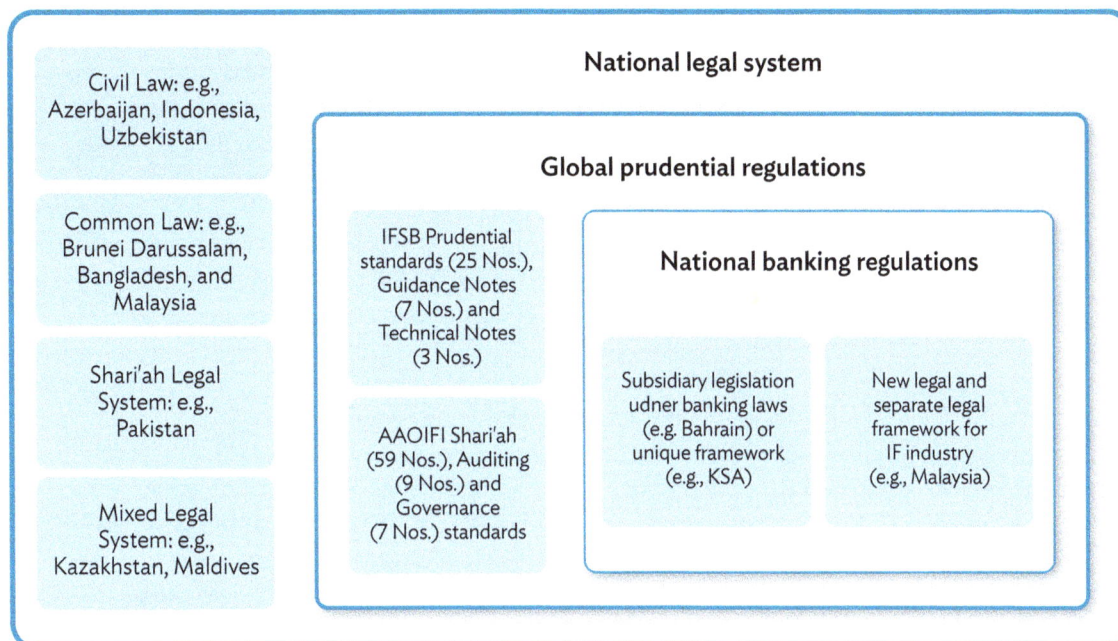

National legal system

Civil Law: e.g., Azerbaijan, Indonesia, Uzbekistan

Common Law: e.g., Brunei Darussalam, Bangladesh, and Malaysia

Shari'ah Legal System: e.g., Pakistan

Mixed Legal System: e.g., Kazakhstan, Maldives

Global prudential regulations

IFSB Prudential standards (25 Nos.), Guidance Notes (7 Nos.) and Technical Notes (3 Nos.)

AAOIFI Shari'ah (59 Nos.), Auditing (9 Nos.) and Governance (7 Nos.) standards

National banking regulations

Subsidiary legislation udner banking laws (e.g. Bahrain) or unique framework (e.g., KSA)

New legal and separate legal framework for IF industry (e.g., Malaysia)

AAOIFI = Accounting and Auditing Organization for Islamic Financial Institutions, IF = Islamic finance, IFSB = Islamic Financial Services Board, KSA = Kingdom of Saudi Arabia.
Source: Asian Development Bank.

Currently, the main prudential regulations for the industry are published by the Bahrain-based Accounting and Auditing Organization for Islamic Financial Institutions (AAOIFI) and the Malaysia-based IFSB—both of which are yet to issue Shari'ah, governance or auditing standards specific to the IFSI industry in relation to the Paris Agreement. However, they have recognized the importance of the sustainable finance agenda and have initiated consultations among members to gradually adopt global sustainable finance, and possibly climate finance standards, in IFSI. Among ADB DMCs, Kyrgyz Republic and Pakistan have adopted fully or partially AAOIFI standards to regulate the IFSI institutions. AAOIFI has started drafting a sustainability governance standard, which is expected to discuss global climate regulations and related governance issues, but until now no standard strictly regulating the climate-related obligations of the IFSI institutions is under consideration.[47]

On the other hand, Malaysia and Indonesia follow IFSB standards, and a few institutions such as the Astana Financial Services Authority in Kazakhstan, the State Bank of Pakistan, or the Monetary Authority of Brunei Darussalam are members of both AAOIFI and IFSB. IFSB has identified the need to capture climate risk exposures and vulnerabilities of financial institutions[48] and is seeking to develop standards in that regard but such standards have not yet been issued. However, there is generally higher awareness of climate risks in Malaysia and Indonesia compared to other countries, which can be seen through their sustainability-related policy development, regulatory efforts, green capital market issuances, and numerous other efforts that align the countries' vision with the global transition to low-carbon economy. This is further supported by an industry survey revealing that IFSI institutions in both Malaysia and Indonesia

---

[47] Interview with AAOIFI executive management, July 2021.
[48] See e.g. Opening Remarks by the Secretary-General of the IFSB at the 14th IFSB Summit 2019 (accessed at https://www.ifsb.org/press_full.php?id=503&submit=more)

are developing internal policies to limit exposure to physical or transition climate risks. This is also a finding of the RFI foundation reports on Climate Risks Facing Malaysia's[49] and Indonesia's[50] Financial Systems.

In countries such as Kazakhstan, where Islamic banking has been formally introduced through amendment of regulations relative to conventional banking (in particular the tax code) to provide a level playing field for Islamic and conventional banking transactions, the adoption of governance regulations with regard to climate commitments under the Paris Agreement is expected to accelerate through the passing of legislative acts recently enacted such as "the Law on Energy Saving and Energy Efficiency," or "the Law on Supporting the Use of Renewable Energy Sources." However, such legislative acts are not expected to transform the IFSI industry and achieve the Paris Agreement objective of "making finance flows consistent with a pathway toward low greenhouse gas (GHG) emissions and climate-resilient development" unless strict regulations are adopted for IFSI institutions to provide value addition through channels such as differentiated offering for low GHG emission and climate-resilient investments.

In other countries where specific IFSI regulations exist, the potential to focus the IFSI industry into financing low GHG emission and climate-resilient development is great but the development of new Shari'ah, governance and accounting standards will probably take several years. Accordingly, the transition will be two-staged as is currently observed in mature IFSI markets: a current voluntary transition of selected IFSI players toward the adoption of global standards (such as Principles for Responsible Investment [PRI] or TCFD) to transition to sustainable and responsible finance independently from Shari'ah governance, and following the development of new standards by IFSI standard-setting institutions in the next few years, a compulsory compliance to these new standards by all IFSI players through market regulation.

In practice, despite the relatively slow development of climate-related Shari'ah standards by the leading standard-setting institutions, multiple banks have individually and voluntarily committed to global climate standards, in particular reporting standards recommended by the Task Force of on Climate-related Financial Disclosures (TCFD reporting) of the Financial Stability Board. In Malaysia for example, in line with the 2018 recommendations of Bursa Malaysia, the largest Islamic banks (e.g., Maybank, CIMB, HSBC Amanah) publish annual TCFD disclosures.

In addition, as identified in IsDB's climate change policy, there is a crucial need to an immediate raising of **awareness of physical and transition climate risks** across the industry. The structural difference of the underlying contracts used in the IFSI results in a different risk profile as compared to its conventional counterpart. Since most of the contracts are linked to real assets, IFSI is generally more exposed to market risks than conventional counterparts.[51] Proper attention to the additional market risks, or even credit, liquidity and operational and reputational risks caused by climate change in each specific jurisdiction or sector would add much to the understanding of the inherent exposure of the IFSI to short or long-term climate risks.[52] In addition, central banks and financial regulators increasingly acknowledge the financial stability implications of climate change. Work is underway to integrate climate-related risks into supervision and financial stability monitoring, as proposed for example, in the principles for the effective management and supervision of climate-related financial risks proposed by the Basel Committee on Banking Supervision (BCBS).[53] Such increased risk awareness, and the necessary transparency in risk reporting in financial and operational statements of IFSI stakeholders would potentially drive the industry toward a much more climate-adapted and

---

49 RFI Foundation. 2020.Climate Risks Facing Malaysia's Financial System. London. November.
    https://www.rfi-foundation.org/climate-risks-financial-system-malaysia.
50 RFI Foundation. 2021.Climate Risks Facing Indonesia's Financial System. London. February.
    https://www.rfi-foundation.org/climate-risks-financial-system-indonesia.
51 Ahmed, H., and Khan, T. 2007. *10 Risk management in Islamic banking. Handbook of Islamic banking,* 144. Additional factors require academic attention such as the higher level of exposure to real estate sector in Islamic Banking as well as the physical and transition risks related to commodities such as fuel and products of heavy industries, which are predominantly used as trading instruments in line with the realism principle of the IFSI.
52 Recent publications such as publications of the Responsible Finance & Investment (RFI) Foundation regarding climate risks in Islamic finance markets can be referred to (https://www.rfi-foundation.org/).
53 Accessed at https://www.bis.org/bcbs/publ/d530.htm. A public consultation on these principles was launched in September 2021.

resilient development pathway. Third, there is a need to bridge a number of intra-industry obstacles including the difficulty in adopting a polluter-pays-principle or accounting for carbon emissions in the IFSI market offerings.[54] The principle of accounting and possibly offsetting carbon emissions has not yet been mainstreamed in the industry due to apparent juristic complexities. Currently, no mainstream IFSI product has been developed for carbon emissions trading, and the purchasing of carbon credits from other nations (under Article 6 of the Paris Agreement) or other IFSI institutions is likely to be challenging. In fact, the very essence of the carbon emissions, considered harmful to the planet, normally disqualifies them from any valuation or commercial transaction under the principle that harmful products cannot be licitly traded in the Shari'ah. Therefore, scholars are working on alternative ways to address this juristic complexity, an effort which is expected to require extensive consultations by leading standard-setting agencies.

The DMCs also suffer from the **absence of "common ESG or green taxonomies," i.e., a common classification system for sustainable economic activities or specifically activities that positively contribute to the specified environmental objectives of the taxonomy.** At the global level, the European Union (EU) has probably pioneered the convergence of all member states in a single classification system, the Taxonomy Regulation formally adopted in June 2020 and entered into force in the same year ("EU Taxonomy"). "The Taxonomy Regulation establishes six environmental objectives: (i) climate change mitigation, (ii) climate change adaptation, (iii) the sustainable use and protection of water and marine resources, (iv) the transition to a circular economy, (v) pollution prevention and control, and (vi) the protection and restoration of biodiversity and ecosystems."[55]

Among ADB DMCs, Bangladesh published its Sustainable Finance Taxonomy and Green Finance Taxonomy in December 2020 as part of the Sustainable Finance Policy for Banks and Financial Institutions by the Central Bank's Sustainable Finance Department.[56] The Sustainable Finance Taxonomy highlights the sectoral focus, the priorities among green products for trading sectors, screening and monitoring framework of sustainable finance initiatives, reporting and disclosures, technological advancement inclusion, sustainable finance strategic planning, product innovation, capacity building, and impact assessment. Meanwhile, the green taxonomy focuses on green banking and lays forth a methodology for defining green projects, carbon footprint measurements, monitoring, and developing green bond standards.

In addition, Malaysia, issued its national climate-focused sustainability taxonomy for the finance sector in April 2021. The Central Bank Bank Negara Malaysia (BNM) published the Climate Change and Principle-based Taxonomy (CCPT), which sets out five guiding principles intended to help financial institutions "assess and categorize economic activities according to the extent to which they meet climate objectives and promote the transition to a low-carbon economy."[57] As part of international efforts to meet the Paris Agreement targets, the International Platform on Sustainable Finance (IPSF) has been created in October 2019 with the support of EU institutions to scale up the mobilization of private capital toward environmentally sustainable finance at global level, and to promote integrated markets for environmentally sustainable finance.[58]

The Association of Southeast Asian Nations (ASEAN) finance sectoral bodies, namely the ASEAN Capital Markets Forum, the ASEAN Insurance Regulators Meeting, the ASEAN Senior Level Committee on Financial Integration, and the ASEAN Working Committee on Capital Market Development, have also jointly issued in November 2021 Version 1 of the ASEAN Taxonomy for Sustainable Finance which is meant to "provide a frame for discussions with official

---

[54] Interview with Islamic finance experts, July 2021.
[55] EU. 2021. Assessing environmentally sustainable investments. Brussels. February. https://eur-lex.europa.eu/legal-content/EN/TXT/HTML/?uri=LEGISSUM:4481971.
[56] Bangladesh Bank. 2020. Sustainable Finance Policy. Dhaka. https://www.bb.org.bd/mediaroom/circulars/gbcrd/dec312020sfd05.pdf.
[57] BNM. 2021. *Climate Change and Principle-based Taxonomy.* Kuala Lumpur. April. https://www.bnm.gov.my/documents/20124/938039/Climate+Change+and+Principle-based+Taxonomy.pdf.
[58] The IPSF is currently working on a common taxonomy for its member states, including Indonesia, which joined the platform (as well as Hong Kong, China; and Singapore) but the regulations have not been issued yet to date.

sector and private sector stakeholders to work together on the development of the ASEAN Taxonomy."[59] To cater to the diversity of the ASEAN member states, the approach chosen for the development of ASEAN taxonomy is multitiered with a common principles-based foundation framework, which provides a qualitative assessment of activities, and a more developed framework as a second-tier with metrics and thresholds to further qualify and benchmark green activities and investments.

Another important intra-industry obstacle to the scaling-up of ICF remains the **availability and capability of human and institutional resources** within the industry to address the climate change in addition to post-COVID-19 recovery challenges, with particular regard to climate risks, climate recovery, and the adaptation agenda. The IFSI players have been generally lacking intra-industry resources to develop internal climate accounting and reporting procedures, which has slowed down the transition of the industry and increased the transaction costs for borrowers and investors, especially for capital markets instruments.[60] With the exception of the current IsDB and AAOIFI initiative to support the development of a GHG accounting framework tailored to IFSI, and the efforts of IsDB to mainstream climate action internally or through the MDB Paris Alignment Framework (footnote 44), no other major initiative has been concluded yet among other IFSI regulatory or standard-setting agencies to support rapid development of internal processes and tools for Paris alignment. The IsDB has also applied for accreditation with the Green Climate Fund (GCF) to be able to extend further support to the IFSI players in adopting global climate action tools and accessing the resources of the world's largest climate fund for their Paris-aligned operations (through green lines of financing for example). The fact that no major Islamic finance institution has completed the GCF accreditation process to date is another indicator of the human and institutional resource gaps in the industry to properly address climate issues.

Finally, the **implementation challenges of the Islamic capital markets instruments are** many and include the absence of a unified regulatory framework and legal documentation,[61] the absence of a unified accounting and reporting framework for climate or sustainability impacts, the high transaction costs for external review, and the difficult access to independent rating of financial products during structuring stages due to low market maturity.

Demand-Side Obstacles

In its 2020–2025 Climate Action Plan, IsDB identifies the second most important objective after raising awareness on climate change issues among market players as the **availability of a sustained and growing pipeline of climate-related financing opportunities.** Due to the realism principle of Islamic finance[62] and Shari'ah-compliance requirements, the demand for financing assets through ICF modalities is expected to be even more restrained than the demand for conventional climate-finance.[63] In fact, recent market analysis demonstrates that IFSI players have been hardly able to finance assets other than renewable energy or sustainable transport projects through ICF products. Even for such projects, the structuring of the transactions, *sukuk* issuances backed by commodities in the stock exchanges through murabahah or wakalah structures for example, poses the challenge of avoiding the use of carbon-intensive commodities (e.g., metals or fuel) as assets backing the transaction.[64] Consequently, multilateral and national financing institutions, including ADB and IsDB, have a key role to play to

---

[59] ASEAN 2021. ASEAN Sectoral Bodies Release ASEAN Taxonomy for Sustainable Finance – Version 1. https://asean.org/asean-sectoral-bodies-release-asean-taxonomy-for-sustainable-finance-version-1/.

[60] Interview with Islamic finance experts, July 2021.

[61] This is partially addressed for the *Sukuk Al Ijarah*, the dominant fixed-income *sukuk* product, thanks to the joint issuance of Sukuk Al Ijarah Standard Suite of Documentation Templates by the Manama-based International Islamic Financial Market (IIFM) in collaboration with the International Capital Market Association ICMA in October 2020.

[62] The principle of realism in Islamic finance is summarized in Kahf and Mohomed (2016) by three conditions: asset by its nature should be able to generate increments, the contractual transaction should be genuine and true, and returns should be factually produced (Kahf, M., and Mohomed, A. N. 2016. The principle of Realism in Islamic finance. *Journal of Islamic Economics, Banking and Finance.* Vol. 12: pp. 13-47.

[63] No specific study has addressed this issue to the author's knowledge and this research gap should be addressed to adequately quantify demand for Islamic climate finance.

[64] Interview with Islamic finance experts, July 2021.

support the preparation of pipelines of climate-related financing opportunities that can be structured appropriately through ICF products. Initiatives such as SOURCE, the multilateral platform for sustainable infrastructure led and funded by MDBs to support the the development of well-prepared projects to bridge the infrastructure gap, and developed and managed by the Sustainable Infrastructure Foundation, or FAST-Infra (Finance to Accelerate the Sustainable Transition – Infrastructure), an innovative data standard and secure ledger aiming at collecting and managing, transparently and reliably, an unprecedented amount of authenticated data to better deliver sustainable infrastructure for all,[65] have the potential to address this demand-side obstacle provided they are widely adopted by public and private finance players in the IFSI industry, and adapted to Shari'ah-compliant financing specificities. Another obstacle on the demand-side is the **market pricing of capital market ICF instruments**, especially in local currency issuances.However, analysis of recent green *sukuk* issuances demonstrates that **this premium observed in green *sukuk* as compared to green bonds issuances is mainly due to premium for first time issuances and to rating of the issuers.** Mature green *sukuk* issuers such as the Government of Indonesia, Malaysian sovereign and nonsovereign entities, or the Saudi Electricity Company (SECO) having been able to issue green *sukuk* at competitive prices.

A third demand-obstacle to the development and scaling-up of ICF in DMCs in the post-COVID-19 context is the **massive reallocation of national budgets** to social and health sectors, and to emergency support schemes to face and mitigate the economic consequences of the pandemics, and the **reduction of public spending in climate finance.** The opportunities to "build back better" and adopt green recovery pathways are unprecedented. Several DMCs have engaged significant resources and efforts in designing and implementing recovery packages but it is not clear to date whether measures and initiatives included in these packages are aligned or misaligned with the Paris targets.[66] For example, as reported by the Organisation for Economic Co-operation and Development (OECD, footnote 63), the tax reduction implemented in Indonesia for electricity bills of poorest households is considered as having a negative impact for the environment while the regulatory change adopted for the environmental permitting process under the Omnibus bill has a mixed impact.

An additional dimension pertains to the **low level of awareness in IFSI industry of the substantial investment gaps in climate risks, climate resilience, and climate disaster management.** The survey of IFSI experts has confirmed that there is an increasing level of awareness on climate mitigation targets. Among the DMCs of concern, the NDCs and revised NDCs reflect quantifiable targets and objectives in climate mitigation that are increasingly imposed through regulatory bodies (including central banks) on the economic sectors including IFSI.

Consequently, IFSI institutions have started developing corporate strategies to align their portfolio to mitigate the risks of stranded assets or reduce exposure to regulatory changes, especially through ESG initiatives (see next sections). However, the adaptation challenges and the substantial needs for climate resilience and climate disaster management investments have not yet translated into regulatory measures in the DMCs nor into corporate transformation for IFSI players.

In addition, some IFSI experts perceive that managing future risks is generally difficult to translate into profitable market products through IF structures. The structuring of risk mitigation or hedging products in IF is limited due to prohibition of *gharar* and third-party guarantees are essentially contributory contracts by essence.[67] Accordingly, although de-risking ICF transactions is welcome to improve their pricing and marketability, such experts argue against the responsibility of IFSI players to propose such products and call upon the public sector or multilateral institutions to support climate risk hedging initiatives. In general, hedging is permitted by the Shari-ah as it fulfills the

---

[65] Climate Policy Initiative. 2021. New Label Designed to Identify Sustainable Infrastructure Assets Launches at COP26. https://www. climatepolicyinitiative.org/press-release/new-label-designed-to-identify-sustainable-infrastructure-assets-launches-at-cop26/.

[66] The OECD Green Recovery Database is an interesting attempt at qualifying the impact of national-level recovery measures (positive, negative or mixed) and identifies 680 measures of environmental relevance for the 43 OECD countries and the Euro. https://www.oecd.org/coronavirus/en/themes/green-recovery.

[67] Hegazy, W. 2007. Islamic liability (daman) as practiced by Islamic financial institutions. Wis. Int'l LJ, 25: p. 797.

fundamental objective of protection of property.[68] Initiatives by public actors such as national development banks and green investment banks to mitigate project-level risks and attract private investment in green infrastructure for example are therefore welcome to boost ICF and efforts to catalyze such initiatives have been attempted recently.[69] However, no sizable initiative of green bank, green fund, or catalytic facility specifically aiming at crowding-in investors into ICF projects or products has been identified in the scope of this research. In addition, the private sector has arguably failed so far to propose innovative products for de-risking ICF transactions and hedging climate risks through Shari-ah-compliant structuring. This will be a critical driver to boosting demand for ICF products in the future.

A key driver for investors focusing on the low-carbon transition are the mechanisms set by countries to mitigate and adapt to climate change on global and national levels. A recent study highlights the central role of the government, the legal framework, and the diversification of green finance and green capital mobilization tools in the green finance decisions of international and domestic investors in South Asia.[70] The financial costs of GHG emissions, the granularity of the stock taking, the coherence of the national climate or sustainable finance policies, and the transparency of the government initiatives are other key factors that directly impact green investors' decisions. Despite many of the member countries having ratified the Paris Agreement and submitted their NDCs, most of the IsDB member countries and ADB DMCs do not have sufficient climate data to track or assess their progress and lag behind in terms of implementation capacity.[71] To attract climate funds and international climate finance, governments must prioritize building capacity and accelerating implementation of relevant policies and tools to attract climate investment.

Box 2. Example of Nationally Determined Contributions among ADB Developing Member Countries

Indonesia:

In 2016, Indonesia ratified the Paris Agreement along with many member countries. The Government of Indonesia submitted its Nationally Determined Contributions (NDCs) in the same year with their commitment to a greenhouse gas reduction target of 29% in comparison to the business-as-usual scenario by 2030 compared to 2005 as a base year. In 2020, the government submitted their updated NDCs to extend the target year to 2050 while maintaining the same targeted reduction of 29%. Although the government has taken several efforts to build a conducive regulatory environment for green initiatives, there is some incongruence in policies such as those that target increasing the share of coal in the country's energy mix and to increase palm oil production. This does not take into consideration the climate ramification. This incongruence may threaten the climate action and green agenda of the country.[a]

Continued on next page

---

[68] Mohd razif, nor fahimah and Mohamad, Shamsiah and Rahman, N.N.A. 2012. *Permissibility of hedging in Islamic finance.* 12. 155–159. 10.5829/idosi.mejsr.2012.12.2.1679.

[69] The State Bank of Pakistan (SBP) prepared for example Green Banking guidelines in October 2017. Each bank in the country is accordingly requested to develop consequently its green banking policies, adapt its financial mechanisms that can allow banks/IFIs to finance environment friendly industrial sectors, incorporate green banking practices in internal control procedures and introduce green exposure limits.

[70] Tran, T., Do, H., Vu, T & Do, N. 2020. The factors affecting green investment for sustainable development. Decision Science Letters, 9(3), pp. 365-386.

[71] https://climateactiontracker.org/

Box 2 continued

Bangladesh:

Bangladesh submitted its NDCs in 2020 targeting a 5% unconditional reduction in emissions in addition to a 10% further reduction conditional upon international investments by 2030.[b] It updated this objective in August 2021 further committing to 6.73% reduction in emissions in the unconditional scenario and 15.12% in the conditional scenario by 2030.[b] Comparatively late in its submission compared to other member countries, the government of Bangladesh has on the positive side been developing a comprehensive regulatory environment for its sustainability agenda which positions the climate-vulnerable country to the forefront of the adaptation agenda in the region. Prior to issuing its NDCs, the Ministry of Environment, Forest and Climate Change launched a road map and action plan for implementing the country's NDCs, a policy document which links the NDCs for each sector with the government's Seventh Five Year Plan (2016–2020) and estimates the budget needed to achieve the targets.[c] As Chair of the Climate Vulnerable Forum, Bangladesh has also launched the "Mujib Climate Prosperity Plan" for the country, a strategic investment framework to mobilize financing for implementing renewable energy and climate resilience initiatives.

[a] Goud, B. and Tabet, E. (n.d.) Understanding Climate Risks in Indonesia's Financial System.
     https://www.rfi-foundation.org/climate-risks-financial-system-indonesia
[b] United Nations. NDC Registry. https://unfccc.int/NDCREG
[c] Government of Bangladesh, Ministry of Environment, Forest and Climate Change.
     https://moef.portal.gov.bd/sites/default/files/files/moef.portal.gov.bd/page/ac0ce881_4b1d_4844_a426_1b6ee36d2453/
     NDC%20Roadmap%20and%20Sectoral%20Action%20%20Plan.pdf

Figure 6 summarizes the main challenges identified in the scaling-up of ICF and its development into a mainstream financial subsector in ADB DMCs. Challenges as described before are both on the supply side and on the demand side. Critical actions and enabling factors to tackle these challenges will be discussed in the next section.

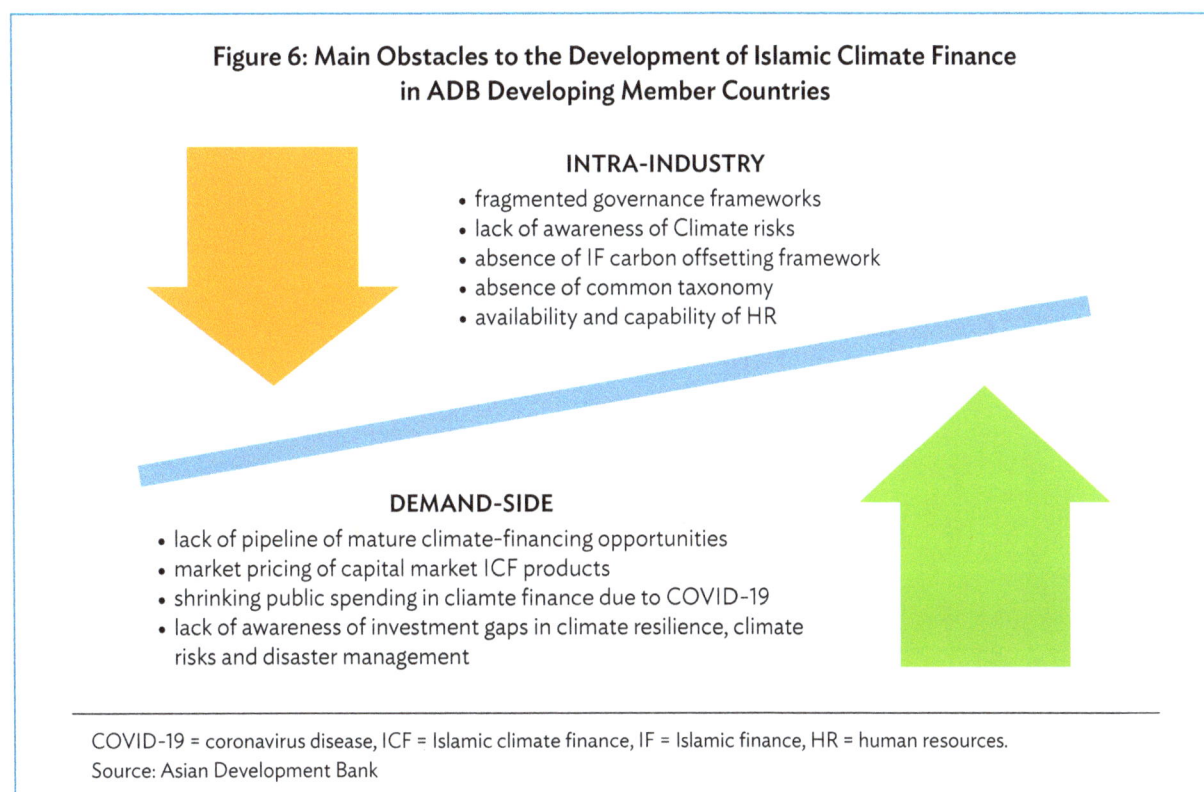

Figure 6: Main Obstacles to the Development of Islamic Climate Finance in ADB Developing Member Countries

INTRA-INDUSTRY
- fragmented governance frameworks
- lack of awareness of Climate risks
- absence of IF carbon offsetting framework
- absence of common taxonomy
- availability and capability of HR

DEMAND-SIDE
- lack of pipeline of mature climate-financing opportunities
- market pricing of capital market ICF products
- shrinking public spending in cliamte finance due to COVID-19
- lack of awareness of investment gaps in climate resilience, climate risks and disaster management

COVID-19 = coronavirus disease, ICF = Islamic climate finance, IF = Islamic finance, HR = human resources.
Source: Asian Development Bank

3 Alternative Pathways to Unlock the Potential of Islamic Climate Finance

3.1 Greening Islamic Capital Markets, an Ongoing Transformation

Environmental, Social, Governance Revolution

While adopting a common taxonomy for climate-related investments and adopting harmonized governance or Shari'ah standards in IFSI has proved difficult in the last decades, **the "ESG revolution" among various investor classes has pushed the IFSI into a transformation pathway that supports a fast greening of the industry.**

As discussed in section 1, the challenges to transform the $3 trillion IFSI into a "green Islamic finance" industry are many (Figure 5). Yet, the industry has embarked in recent years in a major transformation toward sustainable financing frameworks and has adopted the converging environmental, social, and governance (ESG) principles of the responsible finance industry in an unprecedented fashion in the history of the sector. The primary reason for this ongoing transformation is the sharp rise in the application of ESG data to inform asset investment decisions worldwide, and the massive opportunity this transformation of market demand presents for the IFSI.

Figure 7: Market Size and Potential Investor Base of the Sustainable Finance, Islamic Finance, and Sustainable Islamic Finance Industries

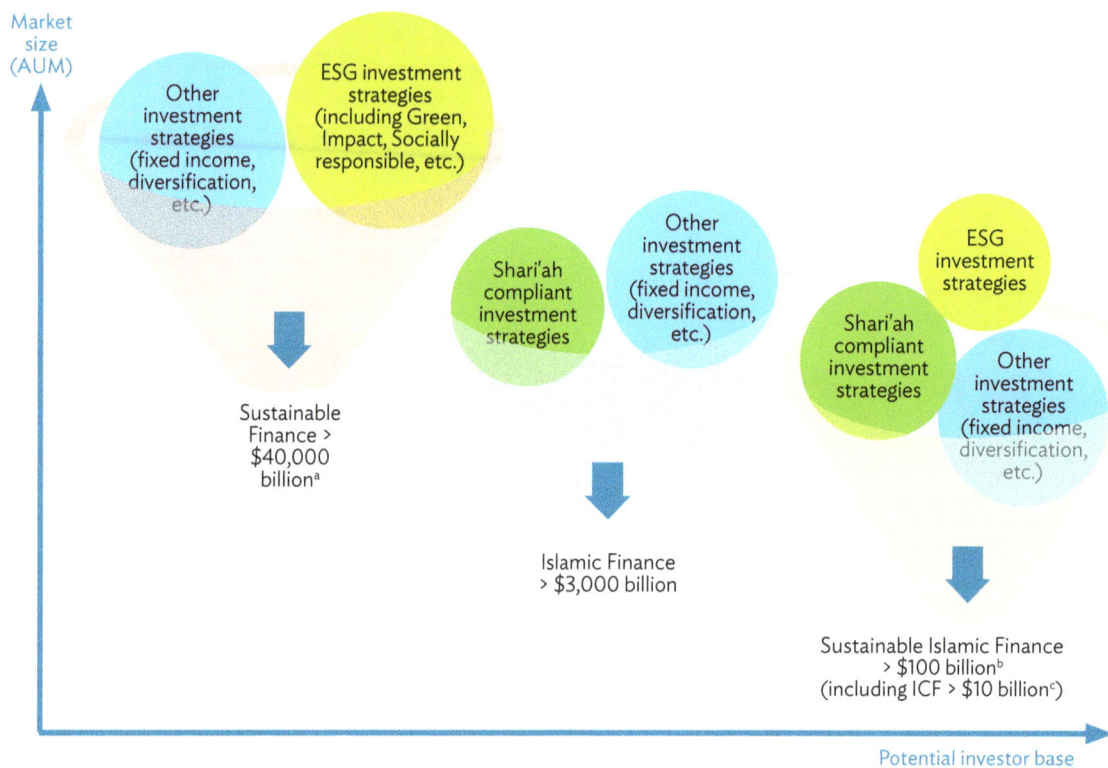

Sources:
[a] Foubert, A. 2020. ESG Data Integration by Asset Managers: Targeting Alpha, Fiduciary Duty & Portfolio Risk Analysis. *Opimas*. http://www.opimas.com/research/570/detail/.
[b] Author's estimates.
[c] Author's estimates.

Global sustainable finance is reported to have more than tripled over 8 years to $40.5 trillion in 2020,[72] with several factors including the changing investor preferences, especially from women or from millennials who are set to inherit unprecedented levels of wealth in human history ($68 trillion in the next 10 years),[73] supporting an even faster transition to sustainable finance from conventional investors and asset managers. Blackrock, the largest global asset manager, declared, in its January 2020 investor relations letter, sustainability as its "new standard for investing."[74] Several major global asset managers have followed suit since and the United Nations Environment Programme (UNEP) Finance Initiative and United Nations (UN) Global Compact report that in 2020 alone, the number of investor signatories of the UN PRI has increased by 29% to 2,701 signatories representing collectively more than $100 trillion AUM.[75] In parallel, major IFSI players (e.g., CIMB, HSBC Amanah, Maybank) have issued their first TCFD disclosures in 2020.

Therefore, the major opportunity offered to IFSI is to tap into a massive and rapidly growing global investor base, which is more than 30 times larger than the traditional investor base of Islamic finance. This opportunity has two immediate corollaries: **the need for IFSI players to quickly embrace the ESG principles of global sustainable finance and adopt relevant policies and strategies to be able to tap into this investor base, and the substantial opportunities this transformation unlocks in terms of market demand and cost efficiency.** This is confirmed by several ongoing initiatives by leading IFSI players and conventional asset managers to mainstream ESG principles in their operations.

In Malaysia in particular, at least six ESG-themed funds have been launched in 2021 alone, while in 2020 only two such funds were introduced. In total, 17 ESG-themed funds are accounted for in Malaysia, but due to lack of local equities compliant with ESG principles (only about 80 of the 1,000 stocks available on Bursa Malaysia), a significant share of these funds is invested in mature markets.[76] Figure 8 presents some of the flagship Shari'ah-compliant ESG investment initiatives that support greener investment strategies among IFSI players. The risks of relying on ESG principles and strategies alone to green the investment portfolios of IFSI players are many (including the risk of "green-washing") and this indirect channel to developing ICF should not be to the detriment of a direct development of ICF tools and products, such as green *sukuk*, green Islamic funds, or green lines of finance and lending products. However, in the rapid transformation of the Islamic finance industry toward more responsible and sustainable investments, in accordance with the fundamental Shari'ah orientation as discussed in section one, should be acclaimed and supported among ADB DMCs.

Four reports recently edited by the United Kingdom Islamic Finance Council (UKIFC) provide an overview of the alignment of Islamic financial institutions with the principles of responsible investment, responsible banking or the SDGs in general.[77] The conclusions of these reports confirm that there has been limited participation from the Islamic finance sector in leading global UN initiatives to promote SDGs in the commercial sectors such as PRI, Principles for Responsible Banking (PRB) and Principles for Sustainable Insurance. Among the challenges identified, the *"overly legalistic analysis of Shariah compliance"* is challenged, since the principles of Islamic finance rather support evaluation of wider societal impacts, through a governance framework which integrates "higher objectives of the Islamic law (*Maqasid al-Shari'ah*, refer to section 3.2), the SDGs and provides direction for how financial transactions should be arranged in an Islamic economic system."[78] The analysis of

---

[72] Foubert, A. 2017. ESG Data Integration by Asset Managers : Targeting Alpha, Fiduciary Duty & Portfolio Risk Analysis. *Opimas*. http://www.opimas.com/research/570/detail/.

[73] ADB. 2021. *Sustainable Finance: A Primer and Recent Developments*. Manila. https://www.adb.org/sites/default/files/institutional-document/691951/ado2021bp-sustainable-finance.pdf

[74] Blackrock. 2020. Sustainability as BlackRock's New Standard for Investing. https://www.blackrock.com/corporate/investor-relations/2020-blackrock-client-letter.

[75] Principles for Responsible Investment. Enhance our global footprint. https://www.unpri.org/annual-report-2020/how-we-work/building-our-effectiveness/enhance-our-global-footprint.

[76] The Edge Markets. 2021. Cover Story: Getting to know the new ESG funds. https://www.theedgemarkets.com/article/cover-story-getting-know-new-esg-funds.

[77] UKIFC. 2020-21. *Thought leadership series Part 1 to 4*. London. //www.ukifc.com/sdg/

[78] According to the UKIFC. 2021. *Thought leadership series Part 4, Islamic Finance: Shari'ah and the SDGs*. London. October. https://www.ukifc.com/sdg/

the alignment with UN PRI shows that only 12 countries (including Malaysia and Indonesia) among OIC countries have institutions signatories of the PRI, and only 1% of the 3,575 global PRI signatories are from OIC countries. Even among these signatories, the absence of unified taxonomy for impact assessment prevents convergence of the sector toward SDGs agenda. In addition, only three Islamic banks are among the 221 signatories of the PRB, and six banks with Islamic windows. The reports call for immediate action by IFSI players to mainstream SDGs and generally speaking societal impact in their operation, possibly through the intervention of Shari'ah scholars who could extend their roles to checking not only the juristic compliance but also the societal impact. According to the UKIFC (footnote 78), the integration of waqf and *zakat* with the finance sector can also play a major role in realizing the SDGs agenda, and the harmonization of standards, the emergence of fintech, or the development of philanthropic instruments can all accelerate the transition toward an SDGs-aligned IFSI industry, a positive-step toward more focus on climate action and green, resilient and inclusive post-COVID recovery.

Figure 8: Sample of Ongoing or Recent Flagship Shari'ah-Compliant Environmental, Social, Governance Investment Initiatives

Islamic Corporation for the Development of the Private Sector (ICD), Jeddah - KSA: ongoing development of ESG standards for private and public sector Sukuk issuances - Due 2022

AAOIFI, Manama-Bahrain: ongoing development of Sustainable finance governance standard: Due 2022

BIMB - Arabesque Malaysia Shari'ah ESG Equity Fund, Kuala Lumpur - Malaysia: Adoption of ESG investment screening technology by Arabesque Asset Management, 2017

Schroders Systematic Investments, London - United Kingdom: Islamic Global Equity Fund combining Sharia lawn compliance with multi-factor investing and ESG principles, 2020

Global Islamic Finance SDG Taskforce - UK Islamic Finance Council in partnership with Her Majesty's Government, IsDB and the State Bank of Pakistan - Longon - United Kingdom: private sector led initiative to catalyze engagement of the Islamic financial institutions with the UN SDGs

AAOIFI = Accounting and Auditing Organizations for Islamic Financial Institutions, BIMB = Bank Industri Malaysia Berhad, ESG = environmental, social, governance, IsDB = Islamic Development Bank, SDG = Sustainable Development Goal, UN = United Nations.
Source: Asian Development Bank.

Sustainable *Sukuk*

According to the 2020 edition of the Islamic Finance Outlook report by Standards & Poors[79] the global *sukuk* issuance market currently stands on an annual basis at $115 billion[80] amounting for about 5.5% of the global Islamic finance industry, with about 70% of the market concentrated in the Gulf countries and Malaysia. On the other hand, IFSB reports open positions of $530.4 billion, which accounts for 24.2% of the global Islamic finance assets as of end 2019 (footnote 5). **Within this growing segment of the IFSI capital markets, new *sukuk* products seeking to align with the ESG objectives, while meeting in part or in full the requirements for green *sukuk* issuances, have been successfully issued by supranational agencies sovereign entities in recent years.** These *sukuk* are marketed as sustainable (or sustainability) *sukuk*.

---

[79] S&P. 2020. *Islamic Finance Outlook.* pp. 13–14.
https://www.spglobal.com/_assets/documents/ratings/research/islamic_finance_2020_screen.pdf
[80] Figures for 2018 (actual) and 2019 (est.) in S&P. 2020. *Islamic Finance Outlook.* pp. 13-14 (accessed 28 April 2021)
https://www.spglobal.com/_assets/documents/ratings/research/islamic_finance_2020_screen.pdf

For example, the IsDB successfully raised in March 2021 $2.5 billion via a five-year sustainability *sukuk* at one of the lowest financing cost in the history of the institution making way for large sustainability *sukuk* by sovereign issuer, and in April 2021, the Government of Malaysia successfully issued the world's first sovereign US dollar-denominated sustainability *sukuk* worth $1.3 billion, with the issuance of $800 million 10-year *sukuk* and $500 million 30-year *sukuk*. The *sukuk* was oversubscribed 6.4 times.

Interestingly, despite its apparent market success, this denomination is not yet found in the literature and the application has preceded the conceptualization. Hence, the specialized literature still uses other concepts such as "responsible finance *sukuk*," SRI *sukuk* or *"sustainable sukuk"* to refer to similar sustainability-driven investment certificates. Conscious about the need to harmonize sustainable finance frameworks at the national or regional level, countries have engaged initiatives such as the Sustainable Finance Framework adopted in the Philippines (Circular No. 1085 of the Central Bank[81]). Regulatory agencies such as IFSB and AAOIFI are also currently developing governance standards for sustainable finance. In Malaysia, the Small and Medium Enterprise (SME) Bank, established in 2005 as a development financial institution wholly-owned by the Ministry of Finance and regulated by BNM unveiled in July 2021 its RM3 billion ($720 million) *Sukuk Wakalah* Programme to meet its funding and working capital requirement and finance the development of SMEs in the country. As part of the Third Capital Market Development Program in Bangladesh, ADB supported the Bangladesh Securities and Exchange Commission to broaden the supply of financial instruments and develop a framework for the issuance of sustainable *sukuk*.[82] In November 2019, IsDB unveiled its Sustainable Finance Framework[83] consistent with the four components of green bond principles, social bond principles, and sustainability bond guidelines and under which IsDB can issue green or sustainability *sukuk*. The framework defines criteria for use of proceeds, process for project evaluation and selection, criteria for management of proceeds, and reporting framework.

The sustainability *sukuk* benefits from several market advantages from a demand perspective, not least the fact that due to its mixed objective structure it readily meets the demand segments of green *sukuk*, social impact *sukuk* and vanilla *sukuk*. In addition, from a supply perspective, it offers more flexibility for sovereign agencies or government entities to issue securities based on pools of assets rather than niche assets in the renewable energy sector only or in any social sector. For mega issuances, by diversifying assets in the pool, the issuer can potentially reduce market risk exposure and proposes a product with more stable returns and less-risky profile that attracts institutional investors or risk-adverse individual investors. Similarly, as can be seen in the latest sustainable *sukuk* issuance from Malaysia including 30-year maturities, sustainable *sukuk* offers a larger potential for long-term financing of capital investments or utilities, including in low-return sectors, that is unprecedented in the IFSI capital markets. The market exchange is also facilitated to the increasing number of signatories of the UN PRI, assuming the right standardization of impact assessment is made in the industry.[84]

---

[81] Bangko Sentral ng Pilipinas. 2020. Circular No. 1085. Sustainable Finance Framework. Manila. https://www.bsp.gov.ph/Regulations/Issuances/2020/c1085.pdf
[82] ADB. Bangladesh: Third Capital Market Development Program. Project No. 45253-002. https://www.adb.org/projects/45253-002/main.
[83] IsDB. 2019. *Sustainable Finance Framework*. https://www.isdb.org/sites/default/files/media/documents/2019-11/IsDB%20Sustainable%20 Finance%20Framework%20(Nov%202019).pdf.
[84] AAOIFI and IFSB have ongoing initiatives to define governance standards in this regard. In addition the convergence of regulations on bonds and on *sukuk* supports the harmonization of impact assessment and external reviews. This standardization of impact assessment is arguably the crux of the matter for the successful penetration of sustainable *sukuk* in the long term.

Green *Sukuk*

Conventional finance has started issuing the first "green bonds" in 2008[85] and it is strictly in relation with this innovation in conventional finance that the emergence of the word "green *sukuk*" can be traced back[86]: "A 'green *sukuk*', in which the proceeds are earmarked to achieve specific environmental objectives, would seem to be a perfect product to connect environmentally focused conventional investors and Shariah-compliant investors." Multiple authors have then emphasized the potential of such products and called upon the governments to engage into issuance of green *sukuk*, in particular after adoption of the Paris Agreement.[87]

However, it was not until 2017 that the first green *sukuk* has been issued by Malaysia in the energy sector, followed by a sovereign issuance in Indonesia in 2018 through a 5-year issuance that raised $1.25 billion. The IsDB followed suit with a successful issuance of €1 billion ($1.15 billion) green *sukuk* with a 5-year trust certificates in November 2019. As of September 2021 (Table 1), a total of 13 global issuers have been able to float green *sukuk* since, for a total of $8.7 billion, with a mix of international issuances (e.g., Saudi Electricity, Perusahaan Penerbit SBSN Indonesia III, Majid Al Futtaim, IsDB) and domestic issuances in Malaysia, under the recently adopted ASEAN green bonds standards.

The green *sukuk* issuances have primarily supported financing of renewable energy projects, but interestingly new asset classes have been financed recently for example in real estate through the government-linked PNB Merdeka Ventures green building project in Malaysia, or the Majid Al Futtaim (MAF) LEED-certified real estate projects in the United Arab Emirates (UAE). **Water project or sustainable transport projects are also backing the diversified *sukuk* issuances of the IsDB or of the Republic of Indonesia.** The international green *sukuk* issuances of Indonesia, MAF, IsDB or the SECO have achieved competitive profit rates comparable to benchmark bond issuances, which confirms that for mature issuers, there is no observed premium for *sukuk* issuance as compared to conventional bond issuance. Additionally, the diversified geographic distribution of the subscribers to the green *sukuk* issued by the Republic of Indonesia (Figure 9) with 29% investors from the USA and 9% from Europe, or by the SECO and IsDB, demonstrate that issuance of green *sukuk* is an effective option to diversify investor pool into fixed-pricing capital market instruments.

---

[85] First green bond issued by the World Bank quickly followed by European Investment Bank and other development finance institutions (DFIs).

[86] Bennett, M., and Iqbal, Z. 2011. *The role of Sukūk in meeting global development challenges. Global Growth, Opportunities and Challenges in the Sukūk Market.* S. Jaffer, ed. https://www.gbv.de/dms/zbw/70296302X.pdf.

[87] E.g. Aassouli, D., Asutay, M., Mohieldin, M., & Nwokike, T. C. 2018. *Green Sukūk, Energy Poverty, and Climate Change: A Roadmap for Sub-Saharan Africa.* Washington, DC: World Bank.

Figure 9: Geographic Distribution of Investors in the Green *Sukuk* SBSN Indonesia III

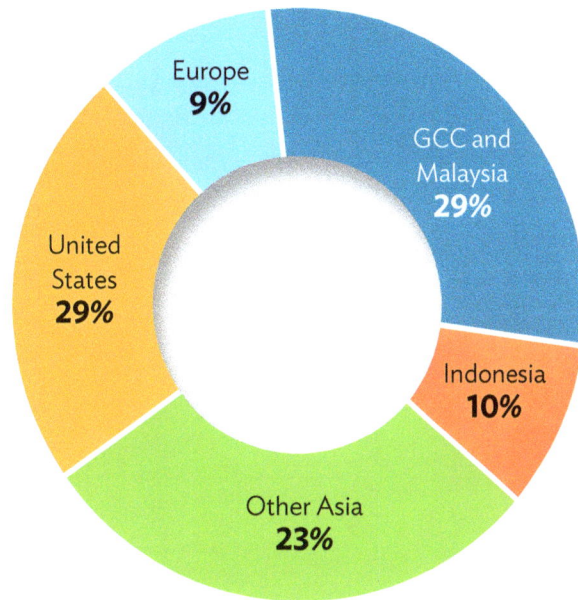

Europe
9%

GCC and Malaysia
29%

United States
29%

Indonesia
10%

Other Asia
23%

GCC = Gulf Cooperation Council, US = United States.
Source: *Sukuk*.com.

The potential of domestic green *sukuk* issuances however has not been confirmed yet outside Malaysia, and despite consistent AA-rating for most issuances, the profit rates remain high and typically above 5%. The domestic issuances are primarily intended for project financing of solar photovoltaic plants (Table 2).[88]

The structures of the *sukuk* vary with a mix of *murabaha, wakala, ijara or istisna* contracts, and for the most part the *sukuk* are issued in multiple tranches with fixed-profit rates.

The second-party opinion of the *sukuk* issuances have been made publicly available by the issuers and demonstrate a genuine compliance to international green bond standards, thereby confirming the industry is mature for issuing green *sukuk* aligned with green bond standards.

---

[88] The ASEAN Capital Markets Forum publishes a comprehensive list of ASEAN Green/ Social/ Sustainability Bonds/*Sukuk*.
https://www.theacmf.org/initiatives/sustainable-finance/list-of-asean-green-social-sustainability-bondssukuk.

Table 3: Green *Sukuk* Issuances Since 2017

Issuer	$ Million	Profit Rate		Issuance	Purpose	Green	SRI	
Saudi Electricity Global *Sukuk*	2500	4,00%	AA-	KSA	Renewable energy	X		
Perusahaan Penerbit SBSN Indonesia III	2000	4,15%	BBB-	Indonesia	Diversified	X		Wakala
Majid Al Futtaim *Sukuk* Ltd	1600	4,50%	BBB	UAE	Energy/Water/Real Estate	X		Wakala / Murabaha
IDB Trust Services	1108	0,04%	AAA	Multilateral	Energy/Water/ Transport/Environment	X		
Quantum Solar Park Semenanjung Sdn Bhd	236	5,80%	AA	Malaysia	3 Solar PV Plants	X	X	
Tadau Energy Sdn Bhd	237	5,40%	AA-	Malaysia	3 Solar PV plants	X	X	Istisna / Ijarah
PNB Merdeka Ventures Sdn Bhd	474	5,80%		Malaysia	Real Estate	X	X	Murabaha
UITM Solar Power Dua Sdn Bhd	60	5,10%	AA-	Malaysia	Solar PV Plant	X	X	
Leader Energy Sdn Bhd	59	4,05%	AA	Malaysia	Solar PV Plant	X	X	Wakala
Sinar Kamiri Sdn Bhd	59	5,52%	AA	Malaysia	Solar PV Plant	X	X	Wakala
Telekosang Hydro One Sdn Bhd	113	5,20%	AA	Malaysia	Hydro Power Plants	X	X	
Cypark Ref Sdn Bhd	130	6,85%	AA	Malaysia	3 Solar PV plants	X	X	Murabaha
reNIKOLA Solar Sdn Bhd	93	4,30%	AA	Malaysia	3 Solar PV plants	X	X	

KSA = Kingdom of Saudi Arabia, PV = photovoltaic, UAE = United Arab Emirates.

Source: Bloomberg, www.sukuk.com.

A Rapidly-Adapting Regulatory Framework

The increasing market awareness on the potential of sustainable *sukuk*, green *sukuk*, and *sukuk* in general has created a large global demand for the fixed-income *sukuk* issuances of the regular issuers such as the IsDB and its subsidiaries, the governments of the Kingdom of Saudi Arabia (KSA), Indonesia or Malaysia, corporate Gulf Cooperation Council (GCC) and Southeast Asia issuers such as the Emirates Group, the SECO, or Maybank in Malaysia (which introduced the first subordinated *sukuk* structures in the market), and niche issuers such as sponsors of renewable energy projects which increasingly turn to the financial markets rather than banks to bridge financing gaps.

This increased awareness and appetite of investors has pushed the industry to rapidly progress in three areas: (i) the rating of IFSI private debt securities by global (Fitch, Moody's and S&P) and regional rating agencies (e.g., RAM Rating Agency Berhad in Malaysia); (ii) the harmonization of the documentation to reduce implementation delays and address investor concerns; and (iii) the pricing of *sukuk* issuances, especially for mature issuers.

The combination of these three factors has led to some of the lowest financing costs through *sukuk* issuances in 2021 for large issuers such as the IsDB or the sovereign Malaysian and Indonesian entities. In 2017, the SECO issued a 5-year corporate *sukuk* of $500 million at a profit rate of 2.655%. In 2020, the two-tranche green *sukuk* issuance of $1.3 billion was issued at a profit rate of 1.74% for the 5-year tranche and 2.413% for the 10-year tranche, despite premium for green issuance.

The regulatory frameworks for *sukuk* issuance have also leapfrogged in recent years, whether in the context of global and regional initiatives (e.g., IIFM, AAOIFI or IFSB standards, ASEAN green bond, social bonds, or Sustainability Bond Standards) or national initiatives (e.g., Astana International Exchange listed the IsDB *sukuk* issuances for the first time in December 2020). In Central Asia, Kyrgyz Republic and Uzbekistan are developing a regulatory framework for Islamic finance expected to address sustainability issues. In a resolved move toward alignment of its portfolio with the SDGs and Paris Agreement, IsDB adopted a Sustainable Finance Framework in 2019, which was externally reviewed and confirmed in CICERO Shades of Green's second opinion to be "in alignment with the green bond principles, the social bond principles and the sustainability bond guidelines."[89]

Moreover, some of the member countries have been proactive in developing an enabling regulatory framework for green developments as parts of their climate actions. In Malaysia, the Securities Commission issued the Sustainable and Responsible Investment (SRI) *Sukuk* Framework in 2014, which highlights the areas projects eligible for SRI. The framework lays out details on the utilization of proceeds, the process for project evaluation and selection, management of proceeds, and reporting.[90] This was a pivotal framework that gave to consecutive sustainability-related policies such as the Sustainability Reporting Guidelines by Bursa Malaysia in 2015 with its amendments in 2018 to support the TCFD. Consequently, the Joint Committee on Climate Change (JC3) was established in 2019—a platform that brings financial regulators and institutions in Malaysia together to collaborate in developing solutions that effectively measure and mitigate financial climate-related risks based on the TCFD recommendations. In the same year, the central bank of Malaysia published the Value-Based Intermediation (VBI) assessment framework, in which a multidimensional risk assessment approach to ESG risks were developed. The VBI framework led to sectoral guidelines for renewable energy, energy efficiency and palm oil, which were published to highlight specific and key transmission channels relate to physical and transition and its impact on financial stability in the light of TCFD risk sources and impacts.

By 2020, the Government of Indonesia issued its green bond and green *sukuk* framework in which a climate budget tagging mechanism was put forth to evaluate and select green projects. The government embedded the tagging mechanism into its national budget system. In June 2021, the Central Bank of Oman issued a comprehensive draft regulation for bonds and *sukuk*, which includes unified requirements for SRI bonds and sukuk and addresses the issuance of sustainable, green, blue, and social bonds and *sukuk* (including waqf *sukuk*) in a comprehensive fashion. Such regulations are expected to profoundly change the ecosystem of the Islamic finance capital market industry and mainstream green, social, or sustainable *sukuk* issuances into global and regional markets.

This acceleration in national initiatives to promote sustainable finance and provide a consistent framework for sustainable *sukuk* issuance is welcome. However, there is a high risk that without rapid harmonization at global or regional levels, through regulatory agencies such as AAOIFI or IFSB or in general through capital market agencies such as the International Capital Market Association (ICMA), divergent standards and legal documentation for *sukuk* issuance will lead to investors' confusion and put extra burden on issuers for negotiation with overseas subscribers. Other challenges for the industry remain, such as the extra costs and processes involved for external reviews, which can be facilitated by subsidies or grant schemes to accelerate adoption of international standards in the market. Financial accounting standards must be developed as well to encourage transparent and consistent reporting of *sukuk* performance while national institutions, in particular public agencies, may play a key role in educating the market by issuing first sustainable *sukuk*, as was observed in Malaysia for example with the recent SME Bank issuance.

---

[89] International Institute for Sustainable Development. 2019. *Islamic Development Bank (IsDB) Sustainable Finance Framework*. https://www.isdb.org/sites/default/files/media/documents/2019-11/2.%20IsDB_SPO_final_051102019.pdf.

[90] Securities Commission Malaysia. 2019. *Sustainable and Responsible Investment Sukuk Framework: An Overview*. https://www.sc.com.my/api/documentms/download.ashx?id=84491531-2b7e-4362-bafb-83bb33b07416.

Figure 10: Main Factors Contributing to the Greening of the Islamic Financial Services Industry

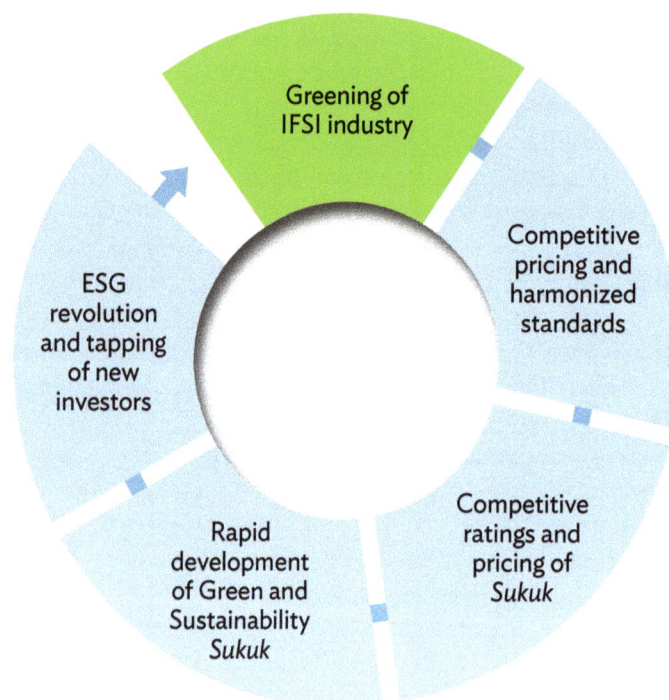

- Greening of IFSI industry
- Competitive pricing and harmonized standards
- Competitive ratings and pricing of *Sukuk*
- Rapid development of Green and Sustainability *Sukuk*
- ESG revolution and tapping of new investors

IFSI = Islamic financial services industry.
Source: Asian Development Bank

3.2 Financial Inclusion and Product Innovation: Islamic Climate Finance for the Unbanked

The level of financial inclusion among DMCs, although rapidly expanding in recent years, is still far from the universal access target. For example, in Pakistan, according to the FINDEX database from the World Bank, less than 22% of the population aged 15 or more are reported to own an account in a financial institution or a mobile payment account in 2017. This percentage more than doubled from 2011 statistics but it is still far from universal access. Azerbaijan, Bangladesh, the Kyrgyz Republic, Indonesia, and Tajikistan reported statistics between 30% and 50% of the population, and within DMCs, only Malaysia reports a financial inclusion over 80% in 2017 (Figure 8).

Coupled with a fast-growing young and active population,[91] **the rapidly growing level of financial inclusion observed across DMCs presents one of the best potentials for the development of sustainable Islamic finance and ICF across DMCs.** For example, based on FINDEX data, in Bangladesh, Kyrgyz Republic, Pakistan, and Tajikistan, in just 3 years between 2014 and 2017, the level of financial inclusion has increased by more than 50%. In Indonesia, the financial inclusion progressed by 35% over the same period.

---

[91]   More than 40% of the population in 2020 in DMCs according to World Development Indicators (WDI) data (https://data.worldbank.org/).

Figure 11: Percentage of the Population Aged 15 or Personally Using a Mobile Money Service in the Past 12 months

■ 2011 [YR2011]   ■ 2014 [YR2014]   ■ 2017 [YR2017]

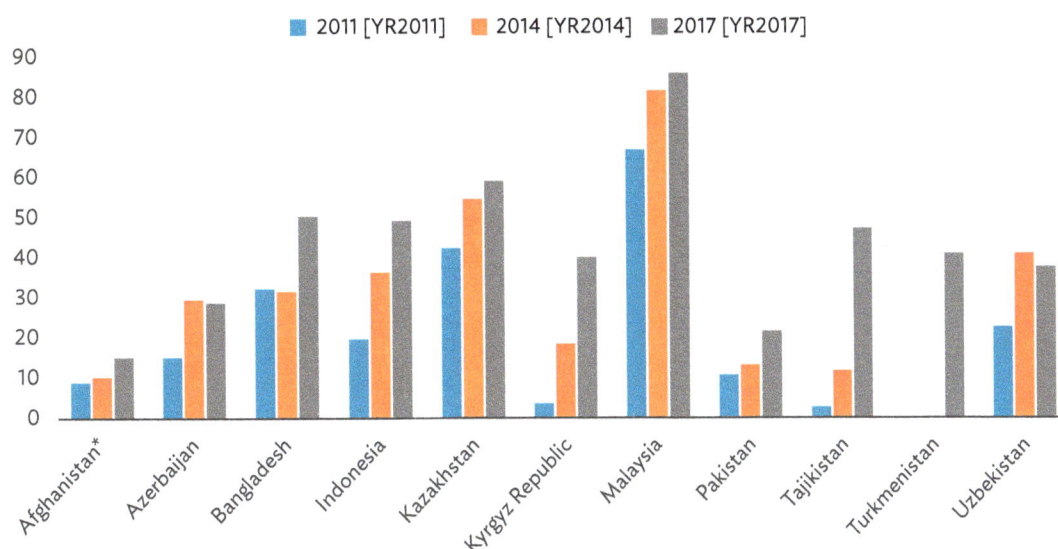

* See footnote 10.

Source: World Bank – FINDEX data - https://globalfindex.worldbank.org/.

On an aggregate basis, with the proper policies and market structures, **a deep financial inclusion across developing Asia by 2030 would directly translate into billions of additional AUM** in the finance sectors, and according to experts,[92] the faith-based Islamic finance sector would potentially attract a significant share of these additional AUM in DMCs with majority Muslim populations. A 2018 survey suggested that half of the global Muslim population could opt for Islamic finance if given a reliable alternative to conventional financial services, particularly in Asia, the majority of this population being currently unbanked.[93] In the context of post-COVID-19 recovery, this increasing financial inclusion offers a great potential to dramatically expand the ICF industry, provided the right enabling factors are put in place.[94]

The role of financial inclusion in helping vulnerable communities build resilience and mitigate losses caused by climate change is recognized and has been further emphasized during the COVID-19 pandemics and the recent climate disasters faced by DMCs. For example, the financing needs of millions of agricultural workers to adopt climate-smart livelihood practices such as agroforestry in the wake of the massive destructions of land and livelihoods caused by typhoons in South and Southeast Asia directly qualifies as climate finance, and ICF products such as cash-waqfs, charities, and donations.

Developing ICF through penetration of the unbanked segments of developing Asia will require the combination of at least three factors: (i) the offering of **dedicated products that meet the ethical expectations** of the unbanked; (ii) the offering of **competitive products** dedicated to the needs of the unbanked and; (iii) the

---

92   Interviews with Islamic finance experts, July–August 2021, ADB.

93   KFHR 2013, in Komijani, A. and F. Taghizadeh-Hesary. 2018. An Overview of Islamic Banking and Finance in Asia. *ADBI Working Paper* 853. Tokyo: Asian Development Bank Institute. https://www.adb.org/publications/overview-islamic-banking-and-finance-asia.

94   A recent International Monetary Fund study concludes that so far Islamic banks have had limited impact on financial inclusion at the global level due to tax and regulatory impediments and shortcomings in the financial infrastructure (Kammer, M. A., Norat, M. M., Pinon, M. M., Prasad, A., Towe, M. C. M., & Zeidane, M. Z. 2015. *Islamic finance: Opportunities, challenges, and policy options*. Washington, DC: International Monetary Fund.)

development of **extended distribution networks** to reach the rural populations and the remote communities, which concentrate the highest proportion of populations excluded from the financial systems. The strategies to develop the ICF product offering can be largely informed by the experience of Islamic microfinance institutions (IMFIs) that have mushroomed in the region in the last 2 decades along the same strategies of offering products meeting the ethical and commercial expectations of the unbanked. While ethical considerations have been central in the development of the IMFI industry, it is also evident that comparatively poor competitiveness of IMFIs on both economic and non-economic factors has prevented their development in countries such as Indonesia or Bangladesh where conventional microfinance institutions largely dominate the market.[95]

In one of the most recent and comprehensive comparative analyses of the IMFIs and conventional microfinance institutions (MFIs),[96] the performance of 101 IMFIs across 33 countries is analyzed[97] and the rapid growth of the IMFI market is recognized. The global market share (represented by financial revenue) of the IMFI segment has increased from $1 million in 1999 to $325 million in 2016, and the market size in AUM has increased over the same period from $9 million to $1,827 million. Despite the variety of profit and loss sharing (PLS) instruments in Islamic finance, the IMFI segment is found to be dominated by debt instruments: 47.6% of Islamic MFI clients are reported to use *murabaha*, 23.1% use *qard*, and 18.2% use *salam*, and accordingly less than a fourth of the clients use equity-based PLS instruments such as *musharakah* or *mudarabah*. The IMFI segment is found to attract predominantly a female clientele with 64.4% of women among clients, an even higher proportion than conventional MFIs (63.6%). In addition, 45.6% of clients are engaged into farming, which confirms the high potential of penetration of ICF in rural areas. Despite lower financial performance, the IMFIs are found in this study to perform better than conventional counterparts in terms of outreach and penetration—although without clear evidence of causality—and the IMFIs are found to serve on average more and poorer borrowers than conventional ones.

The experience of IMFIs has demonstrated that developing dedicated products meeting the ethical expectations of the unbanked and priced at competitive levels can be addressed by IFSI players. However, the challenge of reaching out to poor and remote communities via extended distribution networks cannot be underestimated. Despite solid growth, until today the IMFI segment remains a niche market of less than $2 billion in a $2.88 trillion IFSI that has not markedly addressed the financial exclusion of poor and rural populations in DMCs.

However, the advent of new financial technologies (fintech) in the last decade holds the promise of breaking this major obstacle. In the PRC, for example, mobile payment services have recorded in 2018 alone a total of 60.5 billion transactions, an increase of 61.2% from a year before,[98] although most of the users of mobile payment services are reported to hold an account in a formal institution. In fragile and conflict-affected countries specifically, mobile banking plays a major role in financial inclusion since its development in the early 2010s.[99] Other fintech solutions, in particular mobile payment services or remittance solutions, present a major potential of breakthrough in financial inclusion for DMCs still far from universal access. Among the main obstacles to financial inclusion that fintech can help solve for poor and remote communities include (i) the distance to bank branches due to poor transportation networks, (ii) the complexity of formal banking and long queuing hours in bank halls, [100]and (iii) the significant reduction of financial intermediation costs or the efficiency of electronic know-your-customer (e-KYC) processes. In fact, the advent of peer-to-peer (P2P) payment services has arguably completely transformed the ecosystem of financial intermediation in developing countries.

[95] Ahmed, Habib & Masyita, Dian. 2013. Why Is Growth of Islamic Microfinance Lower Than Its Conventional Counterparts in Indonesia? *Islamic Economic Studies*. Vol. 21: pp. 35–62. 10.12816/0000239.

[96] Syedah Ahmad, Robert Lensink, Annika Mueller. 2020. *The double bottom line of microfinance: A global comparison between conventional and Islamic microfinance.* World Development, Volume 136. 105130. https://doi.org/10.1016/j.worlddev.2020.105130.

[97] South Asia showing the highest concentration of IMFIs with 30 institutions across the subregion.

[98] The People's Bank of China. http://www.pbc.gov.cn/goutongjiaoliu/113456/113469/3787878/index.html (accessed 13 September 2021).

[99] Asli Demirguc-Kunt and Leora Klapper. 2012. Measuring Financial Inclusion: The Global Findex Database. *World Bank Policy Research Working Paper* 6025. Washington, DC.

[100] Makina, D. 2019. *The potential of FinTech in enabling financial inclusion. In Extending financial inclusion in Africa.* Cambridge: Academic Press. pp. 299–318.

The ICF niche industry has not yet significantly embarked in the fintech revolution, but successful Islamic fintech have demonstrated the large potential of technology in breaking through IFSI nascent or mature markets, especially in Islamic crowdfunding (e.g., Launchgood), Shari'ah-compliant robo-advisors (e.g., Wahed Invest), Property investment (e.g., Ethis), investment marketplaces (e.g., Kestrl), payment systems (e.g., Retreeb), P2P financing (e.g., Microleap), *zakat* systems (e.g., IGF) or neobanks (e.g., Mizen, Rizq). In addition, artistic platforms that target Islamic economic activities, such as Gould Studio, collaborated with Greenpeace to connect with global Muslim audiences to encourage climate action. According to a 2021 report, Islamic fintechs are projected to grow to $128 billion by 2025 at 21% compounded annual growth rate, from the current transaction volume of $49 billion.[101] The same report identifies Indonesia, Malaysia and Pakistan as leading hubs of the global Islamic fintech market. 241 Islamic fintech firms are identified as of 2021, across nine service segments, and lack of capital, consumer education, and talent are listed as the main obstacles to the development of the industry.

In parallel, the rapid development of green tech (or climate fintech) in the conventional finance sectors is also expected to drive demand for new digital services and business models in the ICF industry and lead industry into the digital revolution.

Islamic fintech is expected to take a stronger role in economic recovery due to social distancing measures and to the changing consumer behaviors as a consequence of COVID-19. In a recent study on Indonesia,[102] the pre-employment card program (Kartu Prakerja) for example, or direct cash transfer programs to poor households and extensions of subsidized loans for micro, small, and medium-sized enterprises (MSMEs) are identified as opportunities for the government to utilize the fintech industry for post-COVID-19 recovery.

3.3 Role of Islamic Project Financing of Green Infrastructure for Post-COVID-19 Recovery

In October 2020, ADB studied the possible green finance strategies for post-COVID-19 recovery in the ASEAN context. The study identified four criticalities: (i) job creation, (ii) natural capital, (iii) climate change, and (iv) catalytic capital.[103] The challenge on job criticality is to create job opportunities for the millions of women and men who lost their economic lifeline due to COVID-19 impacts, but create jobs that support a low-carbon and climate-resilient economy. Natural capital and climate change have always been critical elements of green economic strategies that are only reinforced in the context of the pandemics because of the substantial pressure on governments to engage into massive public spending packages, particularly in infrastructure, to stimulate economic recovery. Such infrastructure investments must be Paris-aligned and significant support is needed to ensure this alignment despite economic emergencies. For catalytic capital criticality, better prepared projects should be the catalyst to attract increased flows of global green capital, and catalytic funds. These include funds mobilized through the ASEAN Catalytic Green Finance Facility (ACGF), which have a crucial role to play in that regard. Specific catalytic funds could be developed for IFSI. Access to conventional funds should be eased for IFSI players to support the development of a better projects. Government funds available for green infrastructure in DMCs have sharply reduced as government budgets have been diverted to large emergency relief programs and a significant effort is needed in the context of post-COVID-19 recovery to resume and accelerate mobilization of capital for green infrastructure and green growth.

A major segment in which ICF is expected to rapidly develop is **project financing for Paris-aligned infrastructure investments:** 69% of the climate financing reported by MDBs in 2020, i.e., $50.5 billion out of $66 billion, consisted of investment loans, 80% of which ($40.1 billion) financed climate mitigation projects in the energy and transport

---

[101] *Global Islamic Fintech Report 2021.* Salaam gateway.
[102] Sugandi, A. 2021. The COVID-19 Pandemic and Indonesia's Fintech Markets. *ADBI Working Paper Series* No. 1281. Tokyo. https://www.adb.org/sites/default/files/publication/728046/adbi-wp1281.pdf.
[103] ADB. 2020. *Green Finance Strategies for Post-COVID-19 Economic Recovery in Southeast Asia: Greening Recoveries for Planet and People.* Manila. October.

sectors. The demand for climate-resilient infrastructure in Asia and the Pacific is growing, particularly in a context of increasing awareness of climate risks and adaptation needs, and ADB, recognizing that more than 60% of the people in the region work in sectors highly susceptible to changing weather patterns, and that the region is experiencing a sharp increase in climate shocks and stresses, has committed to increase climate adaptation financing. The global estimates for adaptation financing are expected to range from $140 billion to $300 billion per annum by 2030.[104]

At a high-level event hosted by the United Nations Economic and Social Commission for Asia and the Pacific on Financing for Development in the Era of COVID-19 and beyond in Asia and the Pacific,[105] ADB stressed that "Investing in infrastructure that satisfies 'G20 quality infrastructure principles'[106] should be an important part of post-pandemic recovery packages." These principles, or in general the SDGs-alignment and Paris alignment of investment loans fit well with the Islamic finance principles that are inherently toward the justice, equity, accountability, fairness, vicegerency, and compassion. In addition, IFSI financing modalities that are specifically relevant for investment loans in green infrastructure (in particular *istisna'* financing or *ijara* financing) are in high demand by institutional investors and the public due to the long-term financing structures and fixed returns these modalities support. The latest issuances of the IsDB in March 2021 ($2.5 billion five-year sustainability *sukuk*) and the Government of Malaysia's sustainability *sukuk* ($800 million 10-year *sukuk* and $500 million 30-year *sukuk*) are both largely backed by project financing of green or sustainable infrastructure using such modalities.

Box 3: G20 Principles for Quality Infrastructure Investment[a]

- **Principle 1:** Maximizing the positive impact of infrastructure to achieve sustainable growth and development
- **Principle 2:** Raising Economic Efficiency in View of Life-Cycle Cost
- **Principle 3:** Integrating Environmental Considerations in Infrastructure Investments
- **Principle 5:** Integrating Social Considerations in Infrastructure Investment
- **Principle 6:** Strengthening Infrastructure Governance

[a]MOFA. 2019. G20 Principles for Quality Infrastructure Investment. Quality Infrastructure (mofa.go.jp).
Source: MOFA (Japan)

The large-scale mobilization of Islamic finance for green infrastructure financing in the post-COVID-19 recovery requires however two critical conditions. First, the availability of a pipeline of projects for financing through ICF, and second, the competitive structuring of ICF products by the market players, including de-risking mechanisms and incentive mechanisms such as blended finance to crowd-in private sector.

The "SDG Indonesia One" platform was recently launched in Indonesia. It is managed by the Ministry of Finance and by the Special-Mission-Vehicle PT SMi dedicated for preparing and financing infrastructure projects. While not specifically tailored for Islamic finance, it attempts to address both conditions.[107] The platform is built around four pillars including (i) development facilities to support the preparation of projects and therefore build a pipeline of sustainable projects for financing; (ii) de-risking facilities to improve bankability of the projects; (iii) financing facilities, including traditional financing and blended financing schemes, which seeks to attracts commercial banks and private funds into infrastructure financing; and (iv) an equity fund to strengthen capital capacity both for greenfield and brownfield projects.

---

[104] ADB. Key figures in the fight against climate change. https://www.adb.org/news/features/key-figures-fight-against-climate-change.

[105] ADB. 2020. Rebuilding from COVID-19 Requires Green, Resilient, Inclusive Actions—ADB President. Press Release. 31 August. https://www.adb.org/news/rebuilding-covid-19-requires-green-resilient-inclusive-actions-adb-president.

[106] G20 Principles for Quality Infrastructure Investment. https://www.mof.go.jp/english/policy/international_policy/convention/g20/annex6_1.pdf.

[107] SMI. SDG Indonesia One. https://ptsmi.co.id/sdg-indonesia-one/.

ADB and IsDB also share an experience in setting up equity funds for sustainable infrastructure through Islamic financing, with the regional Islamic Infrastructure Fund launched in 2009.[108] Building up on this experience, ADB and IsDB, potentially with other partners, could jointly setup equity funds for green, resilient, and inclusive infrastructure projects through Islamic finance modalities.

The de-risking of green infrastructure financing is also critical since the investment gaps in the region are recognized to be substantial in large part due to risk perceptions by investors. A recent study[109] has demonstrated how decarbonization pathways for developing economies are disproportionately impacted by different weighted average cost of capital (WACC) assumptions. The study estimates in developing Asia a marked difference of 1.7% in WACC between low-carbon (6.8%) and high-carbon (5.1%) energy projects. The Asia-Pacific Climate Finance Fund (ACliFF[110]) established in April 2017 is one of the regional mechanisms introduced by ADB to support the development and implementation of financial risk management products that can play this role, but such mechanisms need to be scaled-up and generalized to massively attract private funds and sovereign wealth funds into green infrastructure financing.

The Regional Infrastructure Supranational Entity (RISE) scheme introduced by the IsDB is also a promising innovation to prepare and develop economically viable infrastructure projects and issue capital market instruments by combining the forces of MDBs and regional development partners, governments, and the private sector into an independent financial vehicle. Under this structure, following an initial capitalization and project preparation stage, project-level long-term funding is envisaged to be sourced by tapping the global infrastructure investors at all relevant risk-return profiles (equity, hybrid, fixed income), thanks to the combination of asset-backed market instruments and guarantee mechanisms by MDBs and governments.

Green infrastructure investments in selected DMCs shall also be coherent with both the Sendai Framework for Disaster Risk Reduction and the Paris Agreement, or in other words shall be in line with disaster risk reduction principles while helping address climate change adaptation needs. This challenge is not yet fully comprehended by project sponsors and investors due to multiple technical obstacles including the difficulty to account for co-benefits of green infrastructure and develop consistent business cases demonstrating the financial viability of green instead of traditional gray infrastructure. This challenge is observed for all infrastructure subsectors, including energy, transportation, water, and urban development.

3.4 Greening Islamic Social Finance

In line with the rapid economic development of DMCs in the last decades, the volumes of social finance have substantially increased, and ISF has quickly developed. According to a recent study by the National *Zakat* Charity (Badan Amil *Zakat* Nasional, BAZNAS) in Indonesia; between 2002 and 2016, the direct contributions through *zakat* or voluntary payments grew on average by 38% every year in the country.[111] Likewise in Malaysia, the *zakat* collections over the last 3 decades have grown by more than 15% on an annual basis.[112] At the global level, UNDP estimates that *zakat* alone could help mobilize $200 billion to $1 trillion annually (footnote 39). In Indonesia alone, the potential is estimated at $22 billion annually,[113] i.e., roughly 22% of the total size of IFSI in the country.

---

[108] ADB. Regional: Islamic Infrastructure Fund. Project No. 42911-014. https://www.adb.org/projects/42911-014/main.

[109] Ameli, N., Dessens, O., Winning, M. et al. 2021. Higher cost of finance exacerbates a climate investment trap in developing economies. *Nature Communications* 12, 4046 (2021). https://doi.org/10.1038/s41467-021-24305-3.

[110] ADB. Funds and Resources. https://www.adb.org/what-we-do/funds/asia-pacific-climate-finance-fund.

[111] BAZNAS. 2017. *Statistics of National Zakat 2016*. Jakarta: IT & Reporting Division.

[112] Department of Statistics Malaysia official portal. https://www.dosm.gov.my/v1/index.php (accessed 21 August 2021).

[113] International Dialogue on the Role of Islamic Social Financing in Achieving the Sustainable Development Goals, October 2021, seminar 3, intervention by Dr. Irfan Syauqi Beik, Director of *Zakat* Distribution and Utilisation-BAZNAS–National *Zakat* Board Indonesia. https://isf.unescwa.org/.

Islamic microcredit institutions mushroomed in developing Asia over the same period, and successful large-scale Islamic microcredit programs such as the Rural Development Scheme pioneered by Islami Bank Bangladesh Limited in Bangladesh have successfully addressed the financing needs of millions of individuals who were left out from conventional microfinancing due to religious beliefs.

The landmark study *How socially responsible investing can help bridge the gap between Islamic and conventional financial markets*[114] theorized the growing convergence of two of the most rapidly growing areas of finance at the global level. The rapid development of social impact *sukuk* and other capital market ISF products has confirmed this trend. The International Finance Facility for Immunisation (IFFIm) may be the first example of such social impact driven *sukuk* issuance with three social impact *sukuk* via the IsDB, which helped raise $500 million in December 2014, $200 million in September 2015, and $50 million in April 2019 for the vaccination programs of the IFFIm fund.[115] Malaysian institutions have then largely contributed to the quick adoption of the concept of social impact *sukuk* or socially responsible *sukuk*. For example, Khazanah Nasional Berhad, the public investment fund in Malaysia, has successfully issued in 2015 and 2017 two tranches of RM100 million ($ 24 million) of a SRI *sukuk* via an independent special purpose vehicle, Ihsan *Sukuk* Bhd.[116] Since 2015, a prolific literature on social impact *sukuk* has then proposed application of the concept to a wide range of social sectors including education,[117] social services,[118] and even migrant support.[119]

In the context of the COVID-19 pandemic, it has been reported that ISF volumes (*zakat* payments in particular) have been particularly high, especially in Indonesia, which ranks first in the Charities Aid Foundation (CAF) World Giving Index 2021: more than eight in 10 Indonesians donated money in 2020 and the country has a much higher than average rate of volunteering.[120] The pandemic has considerably heightened the credit and market risks on the IFSI institutions due to liquidity crunch and risk of bankruptcies in particular (especially of MSMEs particularly exposed during lockdowns), and innovative ISF products may provide an immediate response for governments such as cash waqf *sukuk* structures to mobilize social and benevolent funds at below market rates for financing safety net measures (footnote 119).

Despite rapid growth in volume and in the range of products available, according to global experts, **ISF has been far from delivering its full potential. The post-COVID-19 recovery offers a wide range of opportunities for the development of the niche industry.** For example, BAZNAS estimates that the current *zakat* collections only amount to 3% of the full potential of *zakat* in Indonesia. A large amount of *zakat* is still being collected through informal channels (footnote 114). The potential for *awqaf* in Indonesia could be even larger. The registered land under *awqaf* in Indonesia alone is at least twice the size of Singapore but for the most part not yet developed into revenue-generating activities (footnote 112). Across Asia in general, the *awqaf* properties generally suffer from neglect and unproductive use, while they have a proven record of sustainable impact particularly for local communities and SMEs. The *Awqaf* Properties Investment Fund (APIF) managed by IsDB is a great example of the sustainable impact *awqaf* investment can have in local communities.[121] There is a growing appeal among development agencies including

---

[114] Bennett, M. S., and Iqbal, Z. 2013. How socially responsible investing can help bridge the gap between Islamic and conventional financial markets. *International Journal of Islamic and Middle Eastern Finance and Management*. 6 (3): 211-225.

[115] Interestingly, the time-lag between the conceptual definition in the literature of social impact *sukuks* and the first practical implication has been extremely short, with the first issuance of social impact *sukuk* 1 year only after the article of Bennett and Iqbal (footnote 115).

[116] These SRI are found to generally meet the principles of both green *sukuks* and social impact *sukuks* but do not qualify as climate finance to our knowledge.

[117] Musari, K. 2016. *Waqf-Sukūk, Enhancing the Islamic Finance For Economic Sustainability in Higher Education Institutions*. Papers World Islamic Countries University Leaders Summit (WICULS).

[118] Mohamad, S., Othman, J., Lehner, O., and Muda, R. 2017. Social *Sukūk*: a new mechanism to fund social services. *Journal of Emerging Economies & Islamic Research*, 5(1): pp. 1–13.

[119] Ali, M., Oravampurath, H. B., and Ziyaad, M. 2020. Social impact Sukūk for migrants: an innovative solution. In *Handbook of Research on Theory and Practice of Global Islamic Finance*. IGI Global. pp. 752–769.

[120] CAF. 2021. *CAF World Giving Index 2021, A global pandemic special report*. London. June.

[121] Islamic Development Bank. 2010. *The Development Impact of the Awqaf Properties Investment Fund: A Model for Sustainable Development*. Jeddah. December.

the UN, national development agencies, and MDBs to revitalize *awqaf* for sustainable development. The UN agencies have launched several flagship initiatives to mobilize ISF for sustainable development—the UNHCR *Zakat* Platform, the UNICEF/IsDB global *zakat* platform for children, the UNRWA/OIC Waqf for Palestine or the UNDP/BAZNAS *zakat* programs. A joint campaign of the UN General Assembly and IsDB will seek to mobilize $100 million in seed funding to be dedicated to causes to help accelerate a global response and recovery from the COVID-19 crisis.[122]

While the ISF interventions are increasingly designed in the context of sustainable finance or responsible investment frameworks, the absence of harmonized accounting, governance, or reporting standards remains a major challenge for the industry. **A significant and coordinated regional or global effort should be catalyzed to green the ISF sector, in line with the fundamental principles of Islamic finance and ISF.** In the context of the post-COVID-19 recovery, instruments of ISF should also be coordinated together and integrated with the fiscal policy of the governments.

ISF focuses particularly on the rights of future generations and intergenerational solidarity, which orients most of the perennial charities (e.g., awqaf). As such, they are perfectly aligned with the objectives of a green, resilient, and inclusive future for all, and in the context of climate disasters, the ISF sector has also demonstrated a formidable potential to raise funds for immediate response and for reconstruction efforts with climate-resilient infrastructure. For example, more than 43 million people have benefited from the programs of the King Abdullah Foundation, especially the flagship Fael Khair Program, particularly in Bangladesh, India, Indonesia, the Kyrgyz Republic, Pakistan, the Philippines and Tajikistan.[123] The foundation has notably funded 173 climate-resilient and green buildings that operate as schools but can be used as shelters in case of extreme weather events in Bangladesh as a response to the Cyclone Sidr devastation in southern Bangladesh in 2007.

Similar projects have been funded by other Islamic foundations or philanthropies in response to the extreme weather events in Asia in the last decade, but the absence of coordinated aid efforts as well as the absence of shared governance or preparation standards negatively impacts the efficiency of the interventions. Large-scale partnerships facilitated by international partners such as UN Office for the Coordination of Humanitarian Aid (OCHA) or the IsDB could help channel the Islamic philanthropy more efficiently toward green humanitarian aid.

To green the ISF sector in ADB DMCs, two alternative strategies can be envisaged: (i) a direct decentralized approach where all ISF players are encouraged or incentivized to develop internal tools and strategies to mainstream climate action in their operation and develop specific activities aligned with the Paris Agreement; (ii) an indirect centralized approach where the focus is mainly on supporting or partnering with the leading ISF institutions to align their operations and strategies with Paris Agreement and to improve their collections to channel an increasing share of ISF financial flows. For example, in the context of Indonesia, approach (ii) would seek to support BAZNAS to substantially increase its collections and maximize the channeling of *zakat* funds through BAZNAS (from the current 3%), while supporting BAZNAS to adopt strategies and develop operations aligned the Paris Agreement such as the micro-hydro power projects in in Lubuk Bangkar Village, Batang Asai District, Sarolangun district, and Jambi province. Conversely, approach (i) would seek to support the maximum number of private foundations, nongovernment organizations (NGOs) or local *zakat* institutions to mainstream climate action in their operations and adopt internal tools and strategies to improve their climate-impact. Advocacy campaigns, awareness programs specifically addressed to Islamic NGOs and philanthropies, calls to action by scholars and religious leaders, as well as targeted educational programs can support such initiatives. The leadership of ISF sector in each country is also important to lead by example for the smaller institutions to accelerate aligning their interventions with climate action and a green, resilient and inclusive post-COVID-19 recovery agenda.

---

[122] Proposed joint Islamic social financing op-ed article by the UN and IsDB.

[123] King Abdullah Humanitarian Foundation. The Project To Combat COVID-19 Continues To Assist Benefited Countries As Part Of "Fael Khair" Program. King Abdullah Humanitarian Foundation. The Project To Combat COVID-19 Continues To Assist Benefited Countries As Part Of "Fael Khair" Program. https://kingabdullahfoundation.org/en/the-project-to-combat-covid-19-continues-to-assist-benefited-countries-as-part-of-fael-khair-program/.

Figure 12: Alternative Strategies to Green the Islamic Social Finance Sector

Decentralized approach

Centralized approach

Encourage local ISF players to contribute to climate action through advocacy, awareness programs, targeted educational programs, calls to action by secular and religious leaders, etc.

Support national ISF Institutions to (a) improve their collection and formalize ISF sector with support from government, and (b) adopt and impelment Paris-aligned strategies and programs and build internal capabilities.

ISF = Islamic social finance.
Source: Asian Development Bank

All ADB DMCs can potentially support the emergence of leading institutions in the ISF sector that are championing climate action and green, resilient, and inclusive recovery. Piloting successful initiatives with leading ISF institutions would potentially support in the long run a greening of the whole ISF sector through leadership by example. The direct decentralized approach, which would seek to encourage or incentivize all ISF players directly to adopt greener strategies and operations, should also be studied since it is more in line with the cultural habits of Muslim philanthropists who generally prefer informal channels and direct channels for the distribution of *zakat* and charities. However, it would be very constrained by the large disparity of civil society organizations active in the ISF sector, and their capacity and readiness to adopt climate action principles in their strategies and operations.

3.5 Unlocking Islamic Finance Potential for Climate Mitigation, Adaptation and Resilience

This section has discussed four main channels to mobilize Islamic finance for climate action and a green, resilient, and inclusive post-COVID-19 recovery among ADB DMCs. Figure 13 summarizes some of the critical initiatives to achieve the significant potential of these four different channels. The next section will discuss implementation strategies that can be used to overcome the main obstacles to the realization of their potential.

Figure 13: Summary of the Four Main Potential Channels and Strategic Initiatives to Mobilize Islamic Finance to Support Green, Resilient, And Inclusive Recovery

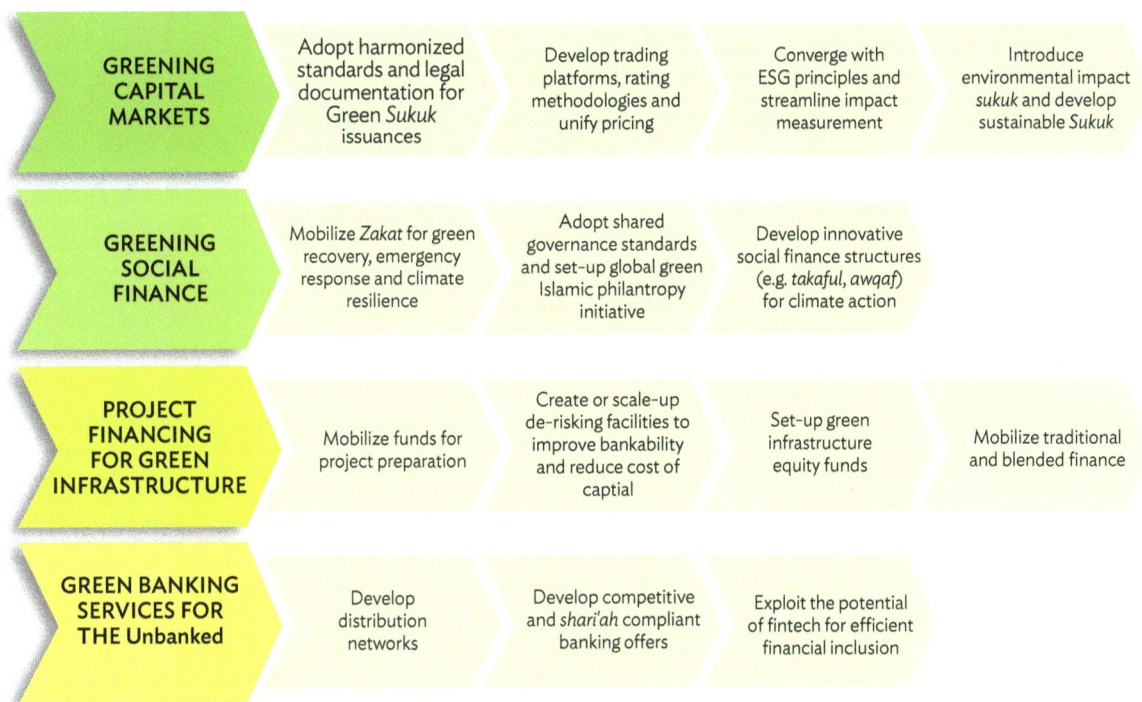

GREENING CAPITAL MARKETS	Adopt harmonized standards and legal documentation for Green *Sukuk* issuances	Develop trading platforms, rating methodologies and unify pricing	Converge with ESG principles and streamline impact measurement	Introduce environmental impact *sukuk* and develop sustainable *Sukuk*
GREENING SOCIAL FINANCE	Mobilize *Zakat* for green recovery, emergency response and climate resilience	Adopt shared governance standards and set-up global green Islamic philantropy initiative	Develop innovative social finance structures (e.g. *takaful, awqaf*) for climate action	
PROJECT FINANCING FOR GREEN INFRASTRUCTURE	Mobilize funds for project preparation	Create or scale-up de-risking facilities to improve bankability and reduce cost of captial	Set-up green infrastructure equity funds	Mobilize traditional and blended finance
GREEN BANKING SERVICES FOR THE Unbanked	Develop distribution networks	Develop competitive and *shari'ah* compliant banking offers	Exploit the potential of fintech for efficient financial inclusion	

ESG = environmental, social, and governance.
Source: Asian Development Bank.

The four channels proposed are complementary in their potential impact to support the mitigation, adaptation, and resilience agenda.

For example, greening Islamic capital markets has so far mostly supported the climate change mitigation agenda with a majority of green *sukuk* directed toward renewable energy projects, in particular in Indonesia and Malaysia. Green *sukuk* issuances in the transport and real estate sectors are also expected to support the mitigation agenda through financing of public transport and electric mobility, and through the support to green building development and sustainable real estate developments (see section 4.3). The development of green infrastructure financing using Islamic modes of finance is also expected to attract investors into climate mitigation projects in the energy, transport, water and sanitation, urban development or agriculture sectors. The asset intensity of these sectors is well-adapted to the structuring of asset-financing through Islamic finance modalities, and from the supply side, Islamic finance institutions, in particular IsDB, have structured relevant modes of finance for long-term infrastructure projects, through *istisna,' ijarah or restricted mudarabah* modalities for example (see section 4.4).

Islamic finance can potentially unlock a vast supply of climate financing for the adaptation and resilience agenda as well. Targeted investments in climate-adapted infrastructure or agricultural programs for example are highly needed in climate-vulnerable regions such as coastal lowland areas or arid and semi-arid regions. In addition, the promotion of financial inclusion through the development of Islamic consumer finance across common member countries is essential for resilience to climate change and for tackling the disproportionate impacts of climate disasters on disadvantaged groups.[124] Pastoralists or farmers are heavily impacted by the impacts of climate change across common member countries and the additionality of pro-poor and targeted ISF programs is essential to address these impacts. Through targeting poor populations with no or low access to formal financial services, *zakat* or charity programs for example can help reduce the exposure of disadvantaged social groups to the impacts of climate change through targeted climate-smart investments (whether at the community or household level) and add the same address consequences of climate disasters through emergency support and humanitarian aid. *Awqaf* or Islamic microfinance also have a critical role to play to increase resilience of communities to climate change impacts and support adaptation of the local economies. Greening ISF and providing Islamic banking services to the unbanked are therefore two primary channels for climate adaptation and climate resilience of common member countries.

---

[124]   Islam, N., & Winkel, J. 2017. *Climate change and social inequality.* New York: UN/DESA.

4 Implementation Strategies

4.1 Post-COVID-19 Recovery Challenges

The COVID-19 pandemic took the world by surprise in 2020 and has escalated from a public health crisis into a global economic crisis—reversing or halting decades of economic development gains in the world, particularly in the most vulnerable economies. Out of the DMCs concerned by this study Azerbaijan, Bangladesh, Indonesia, Maldives, Malaysia, and Pakistan have all regressed or stagnated in the overall achievement of the SDGs in 2020 (Table 3). They collectively account for more than 90% of the population of the selected DMCs. In addition, all countries have regressed or stagnated in the achievement of some SDGs in year 2020 and with the exceptions of Goal No.1 (eradicate poverty), Goal No.6 (ensure access to water and sanitation for all) or Goal No. 7 (ensure access to affordable and clean energy for all) the achievement of all SDGs is now at risk.

Table 4: Trends of Sustainable Development Goal Performance 2020 in Common Member Countries of ADB and the Islamic Development Bank

Country	2020 SDG Index Score	2021 SDG Index Score	2021 SDG Index Rank	SDG 1	SDG 2	SDG 3	SDG 4	SDG 5	SDG 6	SDG 7	SDG 8	SDG 9	SDG 11	SDG 13	SDG 15	SDG 16	SDG 17
Azerbaijan	72.6	72.4	55	↑	→	↗	↓	→	↑	↗	→	→	↗	↗	→	↗	↗
Bangladesh	63.5	63.5	109	↑	↗	↗	↑	↗	↗	↗	→	↗	↗	↑	↓	→	→
Brunei Darussalam	68.2	68.3	84		→	↗	↑	↗	↑	↗	→	↑		→	→	↗	
Indonesia	71.0	66.3	97	↗	↗	↗	↑	↗	↗	↗	↑	↗	→	→	→	↗	→
Kazakhstan	69.4	71.6	59	↑	→	↑	→	→	↑	↗	↗	↗	↗	→	→	↗	→
Kyrgyz Republic	65.3	74.0	44	↗	→	↑	↑	→	↗	↑	→	↗	↗	↑	→	↗	→
Maldives	71.1	69.3	79	↑	↗	↑	↑	→	↑	↑	↑	↑	↗	↗	↓	↑	↗
Malaysia	73.0	70.9	65	↑	→	↗	→	↗	↑	↗	↑	↑	↗	→	↓	→	→
Pakistan	71.8	57.7	129	↗	→	↗	→	→	↗	→	↗	→	→	↑	↓	↗	↗
Tajikistan	63.0	69.8	78	↑	→	↗		→	↑	→	↗	→	↑	↑	→	→	→
Turkmenistan	56.2	61.1	117	↗	→		→	↑	→	↑	→	→	→	→	→	→	→
Uzbekistan	67.6	69.8	77	↑	→	↗	↑	↗	↑	↗	→	↗	→	↗	→	↗	→

ADB = Asian Development Bank, SDG = Sustainable Development Goal.
Source: Sachs, J., Kroll, C., Lafortune, G., Fuller, G., Woelm, F. 2021. The Decade of Action for the Sustainable Development Goals: Sustainable Development Report 2021. Cambridge: Cambridge University Press.

According to data from the World Development Indicators (Table 5), GDP has been decreasing in 2020 in 9 out of the 10 selected DMCs for which data is available, with the most serious setbacks in Maldives (–33%), particularly hit by the reduction in tourism revenues, in the Kyrgyz Republic (–12%), in Azerbaijan (–114%), in Brunei Darussalam (-11%) and in Malaysia (-8%). In addition, unemployment has been soaring in Maldives as well (+37%), in Azerbaijan (+27%), in the Kyrgyz Republic (+22%), in Pakistan (+22%) and in Bangladesh (+215.6%). In Indonesia alone, more than 1 million people have been reported to have lost jobs during the year 2020. Overall, for the 123 common member countries, in 2020 alone, almost 2.5 million people have been added to the unemployed population.

Table 5: Increase in Unemployment and Decrease in Gross Domestic Product 2019–2020 in Selected Developing Member Countries

	Unemployed (Total)		% Change	GDP (Current $ million)		% change
	2019	2020		2019	2020	
Azerbaijan	247,519	313,254	+27%	48,174	42,693	(11%)
Bangladesh	3,072,418	3,703,178	+21%	351,238	373,902	+6%
Brunei Darussalam	14,945	16,654	+11%	13,469	12,006	(11%)
Indonesia	4,930,521	5,840,471	+18%	1,119,100	1,058,689	(5%)
Kazakhstan	442,907	449,700	+2%	181,667	171,082	(6%)
Kyrgyz Republic	176,772	215,665	+22%	8,871	7,871	(12%)
Maldives	7,943	10,904	+37%	5,608	3,743	(33%)
Malaysia	677,985	796,397	+17%	365,276	337,006	(8%)
Pakistan	2,538,184	3,089,955	+22%	320,909	300,306	(6%)
Tajikistan	169,214	183,598	+9%	8,301	8,134	(2%)
Turkmenistan	81,690	95,125	+16%	452,314	...	...
Uzbekistan	981,142	1,079,091	+10%	59,908	...	...

... = not available, ( ) = negative.
Source: World Development Indicators.

The long-term effects of the pandemic and its corollary economic and social crisis are yet to be fully comprehended. Due to the persistence of variants to the disease and to the changed economic and social landscape across the globe, the economic crisis is expected to persist and deepen for several years, causing further job losses, deaths and setbacks in the socioeconomic development prospects of the population. In fact, even the decline in SDGs performance reported in Table 3 is likely to be underestimated due to the time lags in international statistics.[125]

As DMCs emerge from the pandemic, governments now face a major challenge in defining the pathway for their economies to recover from this crisis and meet the ambitions of a sustainable development trajectory leaving no one behind and preserving the planet in line with the Paris Agreement targets. ADB and other international agencies or governments have highlighted that COVID-19 recovery opens an opportunity for countries to lay the foundations for a green, resilient, and inclusive future and "build back better." Despite the profound challenges and distress that the COVID-19 pandemic has caused to the DMCs, it may be a unique opportunity to redefine a development trajectory that will ensure a green, resilient, and inclusive future for all. The key elements of a "build back better" delivery strategy can be assessed along five dimensions according to OECD.[126]

For example, Indonesia was not only severely hit economically and socially by the COVID-19, but also hit by climate disasters such as forest fires in Sumatra and Kalimantan in 2019 and extreme rainfalls and floods in Java in 2020. The country's national development planning agency (BAPPENAS) recently modeled that shifting to a green economy and transition to net-zero emissions by 2045 would

---

[125] Sustainable Development Report. Executive Summary: Summary of key findings and recommendations.
https://dashboards.sdgindex.org/chapters/executive-summary
[126] OECD. 2020. Building back better. A sustainable and resilient recovery after COVID-19.
https://www.oecd.org/coronavirus/policy-responses/building-back-better-a-sustainable-resilient-recovery-after-covid-19-52b869f5/

result in an average annual GDP growth of 6% and would create an estimated 15.3 million jobs.[127] The country has therefore engaged in several strategic initiatives.

Figure 14: Key Dimensions for Building Back Better

GHG = greenhouse gas.
Source: OECD.

The first step of any recovery pathway remains to stop the spread of the disease and facilitate access to safe and effective vaccines for all to contain the pandemics. This has been the priority of response packages designed by governments and aid agencies. In parallel, due to restrictions to economic and social activities, governments have put in place stimuli packages and targeted aid programs that have generally been insufficient to limit the devastating economic and social consequences of the health restrictions, due to limited fiscal space mainly.

4.2 Call to Action

Bridging Perception Gaps through Off-Ground Implementation Strategies

As discussed in section 1, **ICF in ADB DMCs remains today in a double-bind as a niche segment of the Islamic finance industry.** While climate mitigation adaptation objectives are widely adopted among ADB DMCs and countries have renewed their national commitments through NDCs or revised NDCs in accordance with the agreed objectives of the Paris Agreement, a survey of the industry in the context of this study reveals that climate adaptation is not yet a priority in the agenda of leading Islamic finance stakeholders and climate action is not

---

[127] Kwakwa, V. 2021. Indonesia can build back better for a green recovery. *World Bank Blogs.* 13 July. https://blogs.worldbank.org/eastasiapacific/indonesia-can-build-back-better-green-recovery.

mainstreamed in the investment decisions in the industry.[128] The survey of Islamic finance experts reveals that there is a low level of awareness of climate risks, whether physical or transition risks, and for a large spectrum of experts of the industry, climate change is still perceived to be mainly about a reduction of GHG emissions. Climate action is generally associated with extra costs and constraints among Islamic finance experts. It is also thought to be possibly redundant with sustainability agendas (e.g., SDG, ESG, SRI) in the context of developing countries, and to the exception of mature capital market issuers of *sukuk* who have well understood the significant diversification potential that ICF represents for the industry (Figure 7), leading Islamic finance institutions do not yet demonstrate an appetite for radical transition to climate-friendly and climate-resilient investment strategies.

Yet, as discussed in section 2, multiple successful initiatives are ongoing or have been observed across the DMCs, in particular with regard to capital market instruments (green and sustainable *sukuk*), ISF, financial inclusion, or the financing of green infrastructure. The potential of a large, efficient, and competitive ICF sector is real, and the drivers of growth are well identified.

The priority therefore is to bridge the gap between perception and market reality both on the supply and demand side of Islamic finance markets for an effective mobilization of Islamic finance resources for climate action and a green, resilient and inclusive post-COVID-19 recovery in ADB DMCs. This is particularly true in countries where Islamic finance has not yet reach systemic importance and where regulatory and institutional approaches may take years to converge.

In addition, there is a need to increase finance of adaptation measures, which amounts for example for only 14% of climate finance reported by ADB in 2020. Most of the climate adaptation projects in South Asia have been focusing on energy, transport, built environment and infrastructure, water and wastewater systems. Meanwhile, there has been no projects in South Asia that target climate adaptation in financial services, manufacturing, industry, trade, or information and communication technologies.[129] This gap can be filled through collaboration between IsDB and ADB.

In this context, an off-ground and selective ICF mobilization strategy with the development of successful ICF schemes in mature markets before mainstreaming in other DMCs seems preferable. For example, Malaysia as discussed in section 2.1.3 has an edge over other DMCs in the development of green *sukuk* and climate finance for SMEs while Indonesia is potentially leading in the development of green ISF. Bangladesh and Pakistan are two more candidates for a rapid development of ICF products and assets.

For green *sukuk* to follow the growth path of green bonds (which boomed from $5 billion in 2010 to more than $270 billion 10 years later) a mature market infrastructure and a diverse and strong investor pool is required. Presently, this cannot be achieved yet among the selected DMCs from the evaluation of current capabilities of the Islamic finance markets. Given the progress realized by Malaysia and ASEAN countries in the last 3 years in the enhancement of the regulatory framework to support green finance, in the development of capabilities of rating agencies, market intermediaries, and Islamic finance players in climate finance, and in the diversification of products and instruments for ICF, Kuala Lumpur can potentially become the primary marketplace in Asia and the Pacific for ICF. However, other potential candidates could be considered, such as Dubai International Financial Centre, which also successfully developed an ecosystem for ICF in the last few years or even New York or London, which, as described in previous sections, still attract the bulk of issuances of both green *sukuk* and sustainable *sukuk*.

---

[128] Online administered survey of Islamic finance experts, July 2021.

[129] African Development Bank, ADB, the Asian Infrastructure Investment Bank, the European Bank for Reconstruction and Development (EBRD), the European Investment Bank, the Inter-American Development Bank Group, IsDB, the New Development Bank, World Bank Group. 2021. *Joint Report on Multilateral Development Banks' Climate Finance.* London: EBRD. https://thedocs.worldbank.org/en/doc/9234bfc633439d0172f6a6eb8df1b881-0020012021/original/2020-Joint-MDB-report-on-climate-finance-Report-final-web.pdf.

By focusing efforts and capabilities of the entire industry toward one preferred destination for ICF at the regional and potentially global level, the Islamic finance players may raise the profile of ICF and attract market attention while overcoming the limitations of the current size of the market as well as the difficulties faced in converging regulatory frameworks and standardizing market standards. After a successful period of "off-ground" development of the ICF industry in such leading marketplace, reimporting and developing the successful products and schemes into specific DMCs would then potentially much more efficient since the industry would have a track record. The IsDB and other leading Islami finance institutions can play a major role to prepare the ground for this second stage of the ICF development.

In addition, industry players may contemplate the introduction of a dedicated international Islamic finance agency, under the model of GCF by UNFCCC, but hosted by one of the leading Islamic finance markets and potentially backed by recognized Islamic finance multilateral institutions such as the IsDB, to channel public resources and international aid toward climate action and green, resilient, and inclusive recovery. Global institutions active in the climate finance industry are still far from integrating IF modalities, and the perception gap discussed above could be more rapidly bridged on the demand side if such institution is initiated with the realm of the IFSI, potentially in partnership with GCF for a rapid implementation of the model.

A successful example of such partnership between a global aid institution of the conventional sector and a leading Islamic institution is the Lives and Livelihood Fund (LLF) initiated in partnership between the Bill & Melinda Gates Foundation, and the IsDB, and funded by six donor partners (Box 3)

Box 4. The Lives and Livelihood Fund, A Landmark Blended Finance Program

Launched in September 2016, the Lives and Livelihood Fund (LLF) is a unique blended finance program of $2.5 billion, initiated and funded by the Bill & Melinda Gates Foundation and the Islamic Development Bank, (IsDB) as well as the Abu Dhabi Fund for Development, the United Kingdom Foreign, Commonwealth and Development Office, the King Salman Humanitarian Aid and Relief Centre and the Qatar Fund for Development. Ninety-five percent of LLF resources are targeted towards the 33 least-developed or lower-middle-income countries members of the IsDB. These include Afghanistan[a], Bangladesh, the Kyrgyz Republic, Pakistan, and Tajikistan among ADB members. These countries are eligible for blending financing with 35% grant portion, meaning the 65% market-based ordinary project financing of the IsDB is matched with a 35% grant of the donors to the program helping significantly reduce financing costs for the health, agricultural or basic infrastructure projects of the LLF. The LLF specifically focuses on operations contributing to SDG 1, 2, 3, 6 and 9 . As of end 2020, the LLF had an active portfolio of 29 active projects across 22 countries, and committed $1.54 billion in financing.

[a] See footnote 10.
Source: Islamic Development Bank. Lives & Livelihoods Fund. https://www.isdb.org/llf.

ADB and IsDB could play an important role in facilitating the institution of such Global ICF Fund. The experience of a successful joint establishment of a $500 million Islamic Infrastructure Fund to support infrastructure development across common DMCs by ADB and IsDB in 2009 can be instrumental in that respect.[130] Such fund maybe thematically oriented toward green infrastructure financing only or generally support the development of the ICF industry as well as promoting green, resilient, and inclusive post-COVID-19 recovery.

---

[130] ADB. Regional: Islamic Infrastructure Fund. Project 42911-014, https://www.adb.org/projects/42911-014/main.

In parallel, there is an urgent to sponsor strategic research, global partnerships and international or regional outreach initiatives to mainstream the paradigm shift toward green, resilient, and inclusive development pathways for the Islamic finance industry. The example of the current initiatives discussed in section 2.1 to support the alignment of the Islamic finance industry with the SDGs agenda demonstrate the potential and importance of such initiatives.

One of the fundamental yet largely overlooked principles of Islamic economy that supports a change of paradigm toward green and sustainable investments and circular economy pertains to the concept of protection, which is inherent to the higher objectives of the Islamic law (*Maqasid Al-Shari'ah*). It is understood that Islamic law is traditionally predicated on the benefits of the individual and that of the community, and therefore protection of these benefits to facilitate the conditions of human life on Earth is the primary responsibility of the legal system. In other words, while the attainment of these benefits is the responsibility of each human being or community, the provision of the necessary protection for these benefits to be sustainable is the responsibility of the legal system.

The scholars have historically classified the entire range of these higher benefits (*masalih and maqasid*) into three categories in a descending order of importance: (i) the essential *masalih, or daruriyyat*, (ii) the complementary benefits, or *hajiyat*; and (iii) the embellishment *tahsiniyyat*. The *daruriyyat* are five, namely faith, life, lineage, intellect, and property. Islamic law, by focusing on the protection of faith, life, lineage, intellect, and property, adopts an inherently risk-sensitive framework whereby all risks and threats to these benefits must be addressed by the law and regulations. But law and regulations are not enough to protect these higher benefits.

In the context of the ICF, an important advocacy effort is hence needed to revive this approach of suppression of all fundamental risks to the achievement of the higher objectives of the Shari'ah and strengthen responsibility of all relevant stakeholders in the protection of these higher objectives. For example, how can investment into assets suffering risks of write-downs, devaluations, or conversion to liabilities due to climate regulations, or assets suffering risks of destruction due to climate disasters be justified in a Shari'ah-compliant framework while the protection of property is a fundamental objective of the Shari'ah? How can investments into fossil fuel power plants be justified in a Shari'ah-compliant framework while alternative technology preserving and protecting life of current and future generations, and of fauna and flora, are available? While protection of lineage (nasl) is an essential objective of the Shari'ah law, how can investments leading to destruction of biodiversity and the environment, to the destruction of water or agricultural resources, and to the destruction of life conditions for future generations be considered Shari'ah-compliant?

Developing new Shari'ah frameworks integrating comprehensive risk-assessments of potential damages to life, lineage, or property specifically seems to be a very sensible approach to a paradigm shift of the Islamic finance sector toward green and climate-resilient investments. This would be complementary to the current effort of regulatory agencies to develop financial accounting standards, prudential and reporting standards and governance standards for the industry aligned with conventional finance. The specific value addition of strict Shari'ah standards ruling-out investments and financial activities non-Paris-aligned would be substantial since this would lead to a radical transition of the industry toward climate action.

As a result of four decades of product and industry development, Islamic finance offers today a wide different range of financial instruments, including for long-term infrastructure assets. The global Islamic capital market is a multisector segment that includes holistic financial instruments, including *sukuk*, Shari'ah-compliant equities, Islamic funds, and other Islamic structured products, such as real estate and investment trusts, and exchange traded funds. Instruments can be structured to be debt-based (e.g., *qard, qard* with service charge), sale-based (*murabaha, musawama, bai-bithaman-ajil, salam, istisna, istijrar*), leasing-based (*ijara, ijara-thummal-bai*), insurance-based (*takaful*) and partnership-based (*mudharabah, musharakah*). There are also products based on guarantee (*kafala*), agency (*wakala*) or service charge (*ujr*). In practice, the industry has developed hybrid products based on a combination of these instruments to match expectations from investors, in particular for example for the fixed-income *sukuk* securities, which started being traded in 2001 and which have reached today a global volume of $538 billion with more than 12,000 issuances globally (footnote 12).

However, the time to market for product innovations in the industry has proven a challenge due to obstacles including the lengthy juristic processes to approve new financing structures, the low risk appetite of investors for risk-sharing structures such as *mudharabah* or *musharakah* (despite providing the widest range of end applications in the industry) and due to lack of standardization of financial and legal documentation.[131] The product innovations expected to boost ICF in the next decade, including for example climate-impact-*sukuk* or green *sukuk* for social finance.[132] Greentech in the Islamic economy have not yet emerged despite the rapid development of fintech or other technology products for the Islamic economy, and carbon trading or ledger technologies are not yet authorized by mainstream Islamic finance scholars. Two of the most promising subsectors of Islamic finance, *awqaf* (endowments) and *takaful* (Islamic insurance), which have a very high potential to support climate adaptation in countries vulnerable to climate risks, require significant effort to conceptualize relevant products and reach good market penetration.

Takaful, in particular, holds great potentials for climate adaptation efforts, especially among member countries that are highly vulnerable to climate change such as Bangladesh, where one in seven people would be displaced due to sea level rises alone. *Takaful* can provide contingency and risk management mechanism in such cases.

Compulsory insurance has long been used to manage risks which are high in frequency and is widely spread across people. In Türkiye, compulsory insurance against earthquakes was established and mandated on residential buildings that are within the municipalities' borders since 2000.[133] Similar *takaful* services or funds can be established to address specific climate-related risks for its respective effects social group, such as establishing a *takaful* fund for farmers to protect them against flooding or drought risks.

Green *sukuk* are among the most promising Islamic green financial products. Despite being widely used to pioneer Islamic green financing, green *sukuk* face several challenges. First, according to our survey with experts, there is a lack of green assets in their portfolios. This is a natural biproduct of the lack of green tagging, leaving governments with a limited pool of green assets and projects available for green issuances. This would improve as more countries implement sustainability measures and improve their climate governance, accounting and reporting frameworks as there will be more green asset tagging which would increase the assets available for green issuances. Building tagging mechanism and climate accounting infrastructure takes time, meanwhile working on them, green sectors such as agriculture has great untapped potential for green assets and could be used for green issuances in the short run to scale up the sustainable capital market.

---

[131] Interviews with Islamic finance experts, August 2021.

[132] Akram, S. 2019. How Islamic Finance Could Save the Planet. OZY. 13 January. https://www.ozy.com/the-new-and-the-next/how-islamic-finance-could-save-the-planet/91464/.

[133] OECD. Catastrophic Risks and Insurance: The Turkish Catastrophe Insurance Pool TCIP and Compulsory Earthquake Insurance Scheme. https://read.oecd-ilibrary.org/finance-and-investment/catastrophic-risks-and-insurance/the-turkish-catastrophe-insurance-pool-tcip-and-compulsory-earthquake-insurance-scheme_9789264009950-20-en#page3.

Second, there is a liquidity challenge among green *sukuk* in particular. *Sukuk* have long been dominated with institutional investors and sold only in primary markets upon issuance and held until maturity. Consequently, many investors are disincentivized from buying *sukuk* due to the lack of liquidity in secondary markets, which constrains issuers with relatively low issuance volume.

The issuance volumes are further constrained for green *sukuk* issuances due to lack of pipeline of green projects. High trading volumes will be crucial for scaling-up the green *sukuk* markets and turn them into a sizable sector with a large impact in the climate agenda. Innovations such as retail *sukuk* could help with this as most of the green *sukuk* issuances thus far have been focused on institutional investors. An example is the first green retail *sukuk* under the Saving *Sukuk* Series issued by the Government of Indonesia in 2019. The *sukuk* was significantly oversubscribed, and its success led to a consecutive issuance in 2020. Such efforts also contribute to raising public awareness regarding green efforts while increasing the liquidity and tradability of the *sukuk*.

The ICF will only be as strong as the climate accounting used. Hence, more policies in line with enforcement of TCFD needs to be developed. Some efforts have been taken to this end. The Islamic Reporting Initiative (IRI) is a growing international alliance between 50 OIC countries that aim to mainstream the implementation of sustainability and corporate social responsibility among the member states. They published their sustainability reporting standard in 2019 highlighting their efforts.[134] Though it is still in the development stage, the IRI forms a great platform to unify the climate accounting across the IFSI and all the efforts to develop a unified green taxonomy for the region.

Moreover, in 2015, Bursa Malaysia established its *Sustainability Reporting Guide.* The guide laid out the requirements and materiality details for companies to undertake sustainability reporting, in addition to extending GRI Standards and FTSE4Good such as reporting direct and indirect GHG emissions (Scopes 1, 2, and 3). Since then, the government mandated all listed companies to undertake sustainability reporting and incorporate ESG governance structures.

Such efforts, though remains to be general, sets the stage and the enabling environment for institutions to take on the transition toward sustainability. This is particularly important in the light of the increasing pressure from international asset owners who are actively increasing their sustainability requirements and efforts.

More importantly, those efforts provide the data and transparency to strengthen the national and international efforts for climate mitigation and adaptation.

4.3 The Need for Sectoral Approaches

An analysis of the current ICF operations across ADB DMCs or at a global level reveal that climate finance in the Islamic finance industry is still mainly about clean energy and renewables. For example, Table 1 reveals that, with the exception, of the institutional *sukuk* issuances of Indonesia and the IsDB, the private issuance of green *sukuk* have almost exclusively related to solar photovoltaic plants or hydro power investments in Malaysia. The two noticeable exceptions of the government-linked PNB Merdeka Ventures green building project in Malaysia, or the MAF LEED-certified real estate projects in the UAE.

On the other hand, **the Islamic banking industry at the global level is recognized to be highly concentrated in carbon-intensive sectors real estate and manufacturing,** real estate alone concentrating about 25% of the assets under management in mature Islamic banking markets such as GCC countries.[135]

---

[134] Islamic Reporting Initiative. 2019. Sustainability Reporting Standard.
https://islamicreporting.org/ireport/wp-content/uploads/2016/02/IRI-2019.pdf.

[135] Kammer, M. A., Norat, M. M., Pinon, M. M., Prasad, A., Towe, M. C. M., & Zeidane, M. Z. 2015. *Islamic Finance: Opportunities, Challenges, and Policy Options.* Washington, DC: International Monetary Fund.

One of the reasons for this high concentration in asset-intensive sectors is the principle of realism, which imposes the backing of Islamic banking assets by real sector assets such as real estate or infrastructure. The development of ICF portfolio by IFSI players will therefore require two parallel efforts:

(i) The greening of the traditional sectors of high concentration of the IFSI industry (real estate and construction in particular);

(ii) The development of climate-friendly or climate-resilient assets backing IFSI products through innovative or traditional IF instruments.

Ideally, sectoral analysis should be conducted at country level to map out and analyze the emissions' concentrations and identify the priority areas for a more efficient and targeted greening of the Islamic finance sector. This can be done in line with the ADB's Climate Change Operational Framework 2017–2030 (CCOF2030), and in collaboration with the Thematic Group under the Climate Change and Disaster Risk Management. Specific sectors can be prioritized through the development of solutions that target high-emitting sectors. Emission concentrations typically follow sectoral patterns and understanding those patterns would enable a more effective transition of the industry. Although the energy sector is typically among the highest emitting sectors in most countries, which may justify the high focus on green and renewable energy for ICF capital market products so far, it is pertinent to look into varying countries' needs and address them accordingly. For example, Bangladesh has almost 75% of their direct emissions concentrated in agriculture, the sector which is also most vulnerable to natural hazards.

There are tremendous opportunities for ICF in the real estate and construction industries, especially given the great technological advancements in the sector in the last decade. As an example, in the GCC region alone, over $1.9 trillion of development projects have been announced recently, and a significant proportion of these projects include green buildings and sustainable infrastructure developments. The $500 billion Neom Future City development in KSA and its flagship project "the Line" have been announced to be built to the highest standards of sustainability and convenience, although details are lacking on how the carbon footprint of the desert city will be maintained to the minimum. The nearby Red Sea Project, also spearheaded by the Government of the KSA, has already raised over $3.8 billion in April 2021 as a green loan and intends to be "100 percent carbon neutral." Meanwhile, MAF, one of the UAE major real estate asset owners, has been one of the region's prominent investors who has embedded sustainability at the core of its group operations. The group established a "net positive" strategy in carbon and water, the path to which was highlighted in the company's Green Finance Framework.[136] In addition, MAF developed a Sustainable Building Policy, becoming the first in the region to achieve LEED and Building Research Establishment Environmental Assessment Method (BREEAM) certifications across their entire portfolio.[137] In general, the share of green buildings has been on the rise across the GCC countries, with 802 green buildings in UAE, 173 in Qatar, and 145 in Saudi Arabia and Islamic finance has contributed to financing these developments. Similar trends are already observed in Malaysia and Southeast Asia in general, and the Islamic finance industry can be leveraged to accelerate the transition of the real estate and construction industries to carbon-neutral and climate-resilient industries.

---

[136] Futtaim, M. A. 2019. *Green Finance Framework 2019*. UAE.

[137] Futtaim, M. A. 2017. *Sustainability | Net Positive: Our Path to A Net Positive Future*. UAE.

4.4 Policy Recommendations to Grow Islamic Climate Finance across ADB Developing Member Countries

Role of ADB and IsDB

Asian Development Bank Islamic Finance Activities

ADB recognizes the potential role of Islamic finance in supporting its agenda of achieving inclusive growth, sustainable development, and financial stability within Asia and the Pacific.[138] Islamic finance is relevant to ADB because it: (i) provides an additional source of financing (particularly for infrastructure), (ii) promotes financial inclusion (critical to poverty reduction), and (iii) promotes financial stability (based on principles of materiality of transactions and risk-sharing).[139]

Box 5. Examples of ADB Technical Assistance Support on Islamic Finance

Since December 2017, a knowledge and support technical assistance (KSTA) will enable responsible growth of the Islamic finance industry as an additional vehicle for savings, infrastructure financing, portfolio diversification, and to promote financial inclusion in the Philippines (Project number 503-25-001).

In 2017 also, the Asian Development Bank (ADB) ADB approved a regional technical KSTA focusing on the development of Islamic finance in developing member countries, including Kazakhstan, the Kyrgyz Republic, Pakistan, and Tajikistan. It aims to assist their governments to (i) develop an Islamic finance industry in a measured, inclusive, and sustainable manner; (ii) build adequate capacity in Islamic finance within the public and private sector for strong service delivery; and (iii) raise awareness of Islamic finance as a viable alternative to conventional finance both for Muslims and those seeking to diversify their financial services options (Project number 49120-001).

Source: Asian Development Bank

ADB promotes Islamic finance via three main avenues: (i) TA, (ii) innovative financing, and (iii) strategic cooperation. ADB provides TA to develop Islamic capital markets, improve the capacity of regulatory bodies, and build the legal and regulatory frameworks suitable for Islamic finance (Box 4). In addition, the bank has participated in a number of innovative financing projects, including a fully Shari'ah-compliant project financing structure in Pakistan to support the development of critical assets in its power sector. ADB maintains strategic cooperation in preparing best international practice prudential standards for Islamic financial institutions and central banks and in facilitating effective cross-border liquidity management for Islamic financial institutions. ADB also participates in high-level committees, including the Core Principles for Islamic Finance Regulation Working Group, the IFSB, and other institutions such as the BCBS and the International Monetary Fund, to develop the Core Principles for Islamic Finance Regulation. ADB also participated in the High-Level Task Force and technical committees to establish the International Islamic Liquidity Management Corporation (IILM), and with which it now has a memorandum of understanding for cooperation and support IILM.

---

[138] https://www.adb.org/sectors/finance/islamic-finance/issues.

[139] ADB. 2015. Speech at the Launching of "Islamic Finance for Asia: Development, Prospects and Inclusive Growth" – Stephen Groff. https://www.adb.org/news/speeches/speech-launching-islamic-finance-asia-development-prospects-and-inclusive-growth.

ADB has long-supported Islamic financing activities. In 2009, ADB and IsDB established a $500 million Shari'ah-compliant equity investment fund, the first of its kind in Asia. In 2011, ADB completed its first Shari'ah-compliant project financing.

ADB has supported multiple Islamic financing publications and information-sharing forums, often in partnership with other key stakeholders in the sector. For example, in 2013, ADB jointly hosted an international conference on Islamic finance at ADB headquarters, entitled "Islamic Finance for Asia: Development, Prospects and Inclusive Growth" and later published a book (by the same name). In 2015, ADB jointly hosted a knowledge sharing and partnership event on "How Islamic Finance Can Contribute to Sustainable Growth in Asia" and in 2016 ADB jointly published the *"Asian Development Bank-Islamic Development Bank Partnership and Co-financing Guide."*

ADB has an internal Islamic Finance Working Group, responsible for steering ADB's strategic direction with respect to its Islamic finance operations. The group comprises members from various departments and is tasked with operationalizing and mainstreaming Islamic finance in ADB, including integrating Islamic finance into ADB's financial strategy in key DMCs. The group liaises with key Islamic international institutions, including IFSB and IsDB, to explore strategic collaboration opportunities. The group ensures that ADB stays abreast of meeting the demands of DMCs for Shari'ah-compliant financing.

ADB has a strong record of ongoing collaboration on multiple aspects of Islamic financing, particularly with IsDB and IFSB. ADB has memoranda of understanding with both organizations.

Islamic Development Bank, Catalyst of the Development of the Islamic Climate Finance Industry

With its AAA rating, operating assets of more than $16 billion and subscribed capital of $70 billion, **the IsDB group is both the largest and the most wide-ranging IF institution at the global scale,** operating across the 57 member countries of the institution and beyond, and with a range of development finance modalities to sovereign or nonsovereign borrowers through to its mandate of multilateral development bank, or commercial finance modalities through specialized subsidiaries.

The IsDB group has been instrumental since its debut in the 1970s in development the IFSI industry across the globe and providing both the capital and the expertise for the setup and development of IFSI institutions in all segments of the industry. Today, the industry is well developed in some ADB DMCs, in particular in the three DMCs where Islamic finance has reached systemic importance (Bangladesh, Malaysia and Pakistan) as well as in Brunei Darussalam, in Indonesia or in Sri Lanka and Thailand. The regulatory challenges for the development of the industry in other DMCs remain important, especially across countries of the Commonwealth of Independent States. According to Moody's,[140] IsDB first set of funding will be a catalyst for the development of domestic Islamic finance in the region. Between 1991 and 2018, the IsDB has extended more than $7 billion of funding through Islamic finance products to sovereign and nonsovereign entities in the region and is currently supporting the development of a legal and regulatory Islamic finance framework, in particular in Kazakhstan and the Kyrgyz Republic, expected to drive growth of the industry in the subregion. The IF industry is not mature enough in the region to expect a material growth in demand for ICF, but selective operations and programs should be piloted with the support of MDBs or other agencies to accompany the countries of the subregion in the first issuance of ICF capital market products and the development of the Islamic finance industry along green and responsible finance principles.

---

[140] Moody's Investor Services. 2019. *Challenges and Opportunities in Global Islamic Finance Industry Stability.* December 2019.

IsDB has been a premier financier of development in Bangladesh, Indonesia and Pakistan, and the group has also funded aid projects in the Maldives, including for climate-resilience infrastructure. Through its alignment with the Paris Agreement materialized in the Climate Action Plan 2020–2025 and the Sustainable Finance Framework adopted in 2019, the IsDB is leading the transformation of the Islamic finance industry toward sustainable and climate-conscious financing. Through its shareholder role in multiple commercial banks in the region, for example Meezan Bank Limited in Pakistan, Amana Bank in Sri Lanka, Bank Muamalat in Indonesia, the Caspian International Investment Company in Azerbaijan, the Innovative Investment Bank in Pakistan, the Islami Bank Bangladesh Limited, or the Syarikat Takaful companies in Malaysia and Indonesia, IsDB can catalyze the adoption of ESG principles and climate-focused strategies in these institutions. At the same time, through the LLF, the Islamic Solidarity Fund for Development, the *Awqaf* Properties Investment Fund (APIF) or other specialized Islamic social finance institution that IsDB directly operates, IsDB can play a leadership role in transforming the ISF industry for green, resilient, and inclusive post-COVID-19 recovery.

IsDB can achieve this catalyst and leadership role in developing ICF in partnership with ADB and other development partners under the similar partnership modalities than for the SDG agenda where IsDB has been instrumental in supporting UN institutions implement innovative ISF instruments (see section 2.4). Engagement with other leading institutions from Malaysia (e.g., Maybank Islamic, Bank Rakyat, CIMB Islamic) or the GCC that have contributed to the expansion of the industry globally (e.g., Dubai Islamic Bank, Al Baraka Group or Kuwait Finance House), with conventional banks with sizable Islamic windows (e.g., HSBC), or with institutional investors with sizable Islamic finance assets (including sovereign wealth funds) will be essential to maximize the synergies in building up a vibrant subsector of the $2.88 trillion Islamic finance industry.

The IsDB has developed some financing modalities that hold a great potential for a scale of ICF in Asia and the Pacific. For example, in 2012, the $100 million Restricted *Mudarabah* Investment Facility with the Industrial Development Bank of Turkey (TSKB) for the development of renewable energy and energy efficiency projects by the private sector enterprises in Türkiye has proven highly successful in mobilizing the private sector for climate transition of the energy sector in the country. In the transport sector, the €150 million Urban Transport Program also funded by IsDB through İller Bank (ILBANK) was instrumental in developing sustainable transport projects across several municipalities in the country. The Restricted *Mudarabah* facility to TSKB or the more traditional line of finance provided to ILBANK have been effective in the context of Türkiye to fund sustainable infrastructure projects thanks to the availability of solid local development banks, which play the crucial intermediary role between international financial institutions (IFIs) and local private sector developers. This structure of financial intermediation could be made possible under relevant enabling environment in ADB DMCs for a scale-up of ICF through local development banks in the next decade.

The IsDB has a track record in establishing thematic private equity funds with international partners to finance development projects using Islamic finance modalities, and dedicated ICF funds could therefore be developed for ADB DMCs. In April 2009, the Board of Directors of the ADB approved a $100 million equity investment in the Islamic Infrastructure Fund, L.P. (IIF), a private equity fund established in collaboration with the IsDB to invest in Shari'ah- compliant infrastructure projects in the 13 member countries common to ADB and IsDB. The initial target fund size was $500 million, of which IDB had committed $150 million.

The IsDB is also a global leader in Shari'ah-compliant infrastructure financing and the ordinary capital resources of the institution could be leveraged through blended finance setups such as the LLF structure (Box 4) or partial credit guarantees (PCG) such as the ADB PCGs of up to $66.5 million issued by ADB in favor of IsDB in respect of IDB's financing of Foundation Wind Energy Projects I and II in Pakistan.

Figure 15[141] prioritizes the main opportunities by segment of the industry using two dimensions: alignment with the Operational Policy 3 of the ADB and implementation challenges.

In the top-left quadrant, the "low-hanging fruits" are the proposed short-term priorities for mobilizing Islamic finance to finance climate action and green, resilient, and inclusive recovery. Capital market instruments such as international green *sukuk* issuances, domestic green *sukuk* issuances but also green infrastructure funds and sustainable finance instruments appear as the most readily scalable Islamic finance instruments, especially in the developed Islamic finance markets (Bangladesh, Indonesia, Malaysia and Pakistan).

The bottom-left quadrant, the "maybe's," presents candidate additional short-term initiatives, but these require further analysis to make sure they are aligned with OP3. These include ESG strategies by Islamic banks, ESG-themed funds and to some extent sustainability *sukuk* for which there is a considerable risk of "green-washing" or misalignment with the climate agenda if the proper policies and tools for use of proceeds, process for project evaluation and selection, criteria for management of proceeds and finally reporting framework are not adopted. Strict governance framework must be developed in the short to mid-term to support the alignment of the sustainable Islamic finance industry with the climate finance principles otherwise there is a genuine risk that the two industries develop in parallel and that the sustainable finance industry misses the climate agenda.

The top-right quadrant on the other hand, represent the "big bets" or in other words the areas where there is a significant potential but at the same time the effort needed to mobilize these instruments to grow ICF in ADB DMCs may be significant and may require few years of product development and investment. The most challenging yet appealing product for example is arguably climate *takaful*, that is yet to be developed as a product application, and where the high limitations of the current *takaful* players in the Islamic finance industry (especially for reinsurance) are such that a rapid scale-up of climate *takaful* into a sizable industry supporting climate resilience appears unlikely in the short-term. As a whole, *takaful* is today largely limited and represent only 1% of the global IF AUM. Likewise, green Islamic fintech have not yet emerged and may require few years before successfully developing, although promising fintech in the area of social finance have demonstrated the appeal of the Y and Z generations for such products. At the same time, the *awqaf, zakat*, and blended finance programs have significant potential (comparatively similar or superior to the potential of capital market instruments) to fund the climate agenda and green, resilient, and inclusive recovery. There is a need to invest heavily into strategic research as well as support programs to accompany the main players in the industry into climate transition and support awareness and outreach campaigns to mainstream climate issues in the ISF realm. Finally, green lines of finance, built upon successful experiences such as Restricted *Mudarabah* financing by IsDB in Türkiye, can open up a sizable ICF segment into Islamic banking if the right infrastructure is put in place. This can be achieved through the creation of global Green Islamic Climate Fund or through the mobilization of development finance as discussed in the previous sections. Green Islamic microfinance is also a potential big bet requiring further product development and support schemes, in particular concessional funding.

---

[141] Adapted from two-dimensional prioritization matrix by benefit-value and cost-effort. See for example https://www.stratechi.com/prioritization-matrix/.

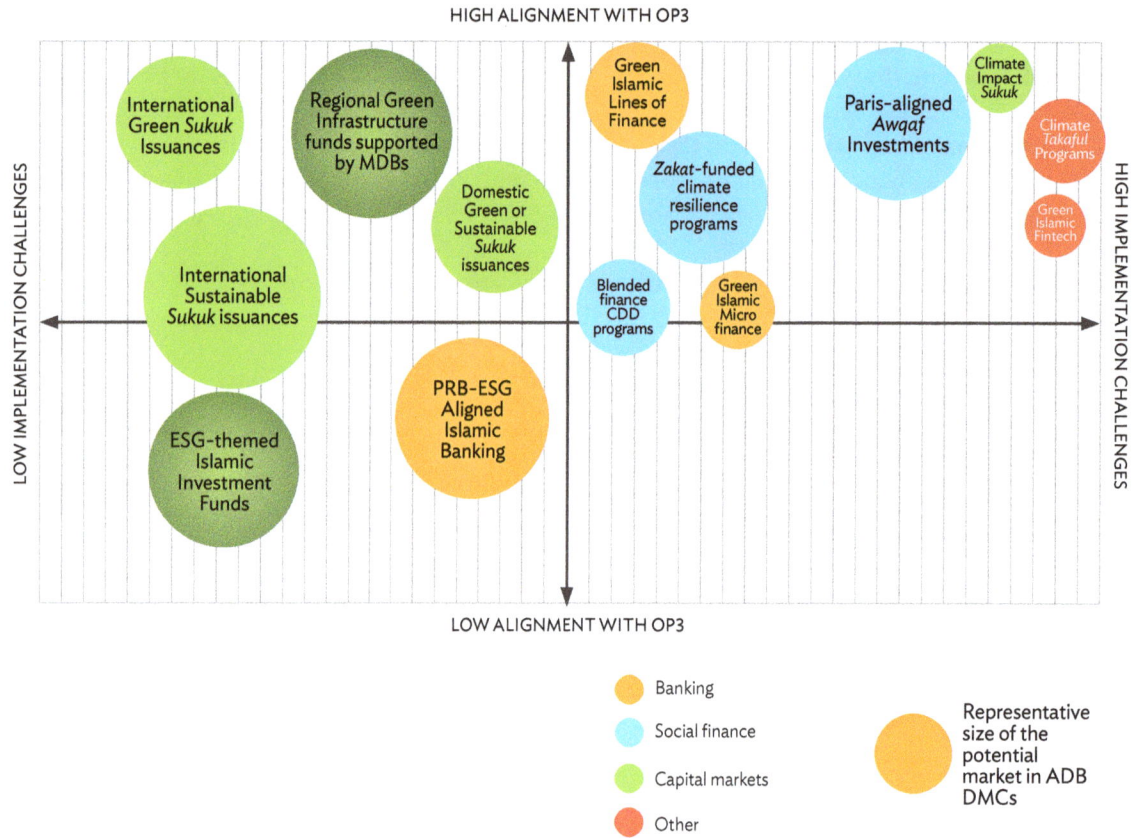

Figure 15: Prioritization of Interventions by Market Segment, Potential, Alignment with Operational Priority 3, and Implementation Challenges

HIGH ALIGNMENT WITH OP3

LOW IMPLEMENTATION CHALLENGES

HIGH IMPLEMENTATION CHALLENGES

International Green *Sukuk* Issuances

Regional Green Infrastructure funds supported by MDBs

Domestic Green or Sustainable *Sukuk* issuances

Green Islamic Lines of Finance

Zakat-funded climate resilience programs

Paris-aligned *Awqaf* Investments

Climate Impact *Sukuk*

Climate *Takaful* Programs

Green Islamic Fintech

International Sustainable *Sukuk* issuances

Blended finance CDD programs

Green Islamic Micro finance

ESG-themed Islamic Investment Funds

PRB-ESG Aligned Islamic Banking

LOW ALIGNMENT WITH OP3

Banking

Social finance

Capital markets

Other

Representative size of the potential market in ADB DMCs

ADB = Asian Development Bank, DMC = developing member country, ESG = environmental, social, and governance.
Source: ADB.

5 Conclusion

This report has looked into Islamic finance and the challenges and opportunities ahead to mobilize Islamic finance for climate transition and a green, resilient, and inclusive post-COVID-19 recovery in member countries common to ADB and IsDB ("common member countries"). The Islamic finance industry has been spreading and gaining systemic importance in various countries across the globe and has developed in a few decades into an industry managing assets worth over $2.88 trillion, including $752 billion in common member countries. Despite supply- and demand-side obstacles, the industry is expected to grow fast in the upcoming years and manage more than $4 trillion in assets by 2025.

According to recent reports, the two countries with the most developed Islamic finance sectors in the world are Indonesia and Malaysia. The Islamic banking industry has more assets under management in Iran and Saudi Arabia but Malaysia and Indonesia demonstrate a stronger performance in the production of knowledge in Islamic finance, in the awareness of products and regulations and in the development of governance of the sector, which reinforce their global position as leaders in the industry. The industry is well developed in Bangladesh and Pakistan as well, and Central Asian nations show a growing interest in Islamic finance, which is reflected in multiple initiatives to adapt or develop national banking regulations to develop the sector. Yet, the development path of Islamic finance in Asia in the post-COVID-19 context is uncertain. The internationalization of IFSI from the traditional markets in GCC and Malaysia has been fueled by two major drivers historically: (i) the improvements in the Islamic finance architecture orchestrated by the setup of global regulatory agencies and standard-setting institutions, which have contributed to quickly setting up regulations and standards for Islamic finance in new markets (including in non-OIC countries such as United Kingdom or Singapore); and (ii) the internationalization of major IFSI players in particular GCC banks, which opened channels or partner institutions in new countries. The internationalization of IFSI players is slowing down in a context of consolidation of GCC banks in their traditional markets, and the industry is facing significant intra-industry and demand-side obstacles which prevent the development of Islamic finance to its full potential in Asia. Tackling these obstacles is paramount to developing the sector and improving access to financial services for the unbanked populations.

Although established under strong ethical and faith-based principles which align well with sustainable finance frameworks and in particular with the climate change and adaptation agenda, **the Islamic finance industry has been generally slow in adapting to the sustainable finance and the climate finance agenda.** Despite successful innovations such as the issuance of green *sukuk* since 2017, mainly for the financing of renewable energy or sustainable infrastructure, the nascent ICF industry remains therefore in a double-bind, as a niche segment of a niche finance sector.

At the same time, the DMCs in the region have submitted or updated detailed NDCs in the context of the Paris Agreement and have started transitioning to green economy and low-carbon development pathways. Indonesia in particular has been leading in this area. Bangladesh also, especially due to its heightened climate-vulnerability, has committed significant efforts to mitigate and adapt to climate change, and has recently adopted a Sustainable Finance Taxonomy. **More countries are expected to accelerate their efforts to "build back better" and adopt green, resilient and inclusive development strategies in the post-COVID-19 context.**

Based on the analysis of this report and interviews with industry experts, **the potential of Islamic finance to support these efforts in developing Asia is confirmed.** In particular four main channels are identified:

(i) Greening Islamic capital markets
(ii) Greening Islamic social finance
(iii) Mobilizing Islamic project finance for green infrastructure
(iv) Developing green banking services for the unbanked to support financial inclusion.

The realization of this potential will require significant efforts which include for example the adoption of harmonized standards and legal documentation, the development of trading platforms and rating methodologies, the streamlining of impact measurement and adoption of common taxonomies, the adoption of shared governance standards for the social finance sectors, the development of innovative products or the development of de-risking facilities for the inception of Islamic funds. The role of international agencies and governments are central in these context to facilitate these initiatives.

Looking at the prioritization of the initiatives, international green _sukuk_ issuances, domestic green _sukuk_ issuances but also green infrastructure funds and sustainable finance instruments appear as the most readily scalable Islamic finance instruments, especially in the developed Islamic finance markets (Bangladesh, Indonesia, Malaysia and Pakistan). Other priorities are identified but require more attention on implementation challenges (for example in green social finance) or more attention on alignment with climate finance principles (for example in ESG strategies and ESG-theme funds).

Given the high asset intensity of Islamic finance, and the concentration in specific sectors such as real estate and construction, developing ICF will require a strong focus of industry players in developing relevant products and financing modalities. Accordingly, there is a need to invest heavily into strategic research as well as support programs to accompany the main players in the industry into climate transition and support the development of relevant products, such as climate _takaful_ or green _awqaf_ or _zakat_ programs for example. MDBs can play a key role in this area, and catalyze the development of ICF in ADB DMCs and beyond, to mobilize the full potential of the sector to bridge climate investment gaps and support green, resilient and inclusive post-COVID-19 recovery for a better future of all nations.

ANNEX: Key Experts Interviewed

Key Expert	Position	Company/Institution
S.M. Aamir Shamim	Group Head – Treasury and Financial Institutions	Bank Islamic Pakistan
Walid Abdelwahab	Former Director General	IsDB (retired)
Suhail Ahmad	PhD Scholar	Sarhad University Peshawar Pakistan
Muhammad Akhtar	BSM	Faysal Bank
Mohamed Alami	Managing Partner (Finéopolis), Former Manager, President's Office	IsDB (retiree)
Ahmed Ali Siddiqui	Executive Vice President, Head of Product Development	Meezan Bank
Mohamed Ali Chatti	Director	IsDB
Shahid Ali Bacha	Project Officer	British High Commission
Jeyhun Aliyev	PhD Student	Istanbul Sabahattin Zaim University
Peachie Aquino	Consultant	ADB
Muhammad Ayaz	Mortgage Manager	ParkTrent Properties
Ahmed Badreldin	Researcher & Lecturer	University of Marburg
Amjad Bangash	Head of Shari'a	Muzn Islamic Banking
Zakky Bantan	Head of Funding	IsDB
Bilel Bouzadi	Assistant professor	ISG Tunis
Seedy Conteh	Finance Manager	QMoney Financial Services
Walid Douadi	Treasurer	Confidential – Former ICD
Mehmet Eken	Senior Investment Specialist	IsDB
Juri Ferrario	CEO	Jfinvestment SA
Blake Goud	Chief Executive Officer	Responsible Finance & Investment (RFI) Foundation
Taoufiq Gueddar	Consultant	Qatar Petroleum / Qatar Government
Mohamed Habib Chenguiti	Manager, Alternative Development Finance	IsDB
Arshad Hayat	Assistant Professor of Economics	Metropolitan University Prague
Mohamed Hedi Mejai	Director, Investment Department, Acting Treasurer	IsDB

Key Expert	Position	Company/Institution
Syed Husain Qadri	Manager Country Strategy and Market Integration	IsDB
Muhammad Ikram Thowfeek	Founder	MIT Global Group
Mohd Sani Moh Ismail	Principal Finance Specialist	ADB
Khalid Jawahir	Senior Finance Specialist	IsDB Institute
Monzher Kahf	Professor of Economics	IZU
Tariqullah Khan	Professor of Economics	IZU
Dr. Mohammed Kroessin	Head, Global Islamic Microfinance Unit	Islamic Relief Worldwide
Arup Kumar	Principal Financial Sector Specialist	ADB
Josh Ling	Fund Manager	ACLIFF
Maalte Maass	Climate Change Specialist	ADB
Omar Mehyar	Lead Transport Specialist	IsDB
Omar Mustafa Ansari	Secretary General	AAOIFI
Muhammad Muzafar Hussain	Credit Manager	Zarai Taraqiati Bank Limited
Muhammad Naveed Aslam	Manager internal control	MCB Islamic Bank Ltd
Daouda Ndiaye	Lead Climate Adaptation Specialist	IsDB
Chingiz Orunov	Managing Director	Ecoenergy Consulting
Waheed Qaiser	Chairman	Pairstech Capital Management LLP / Alephfinance
Nathan Rive	Climate Change Specialist	ADB
Abdul Saboor Gill	Lecturer in Economics	Arid Agriculture University, Rawalpindi
Muhammad Saleem	Advocate	Alnoor Foundation
Haroon Siddique	Business Head - Commercial, SME and Agri Financing	MCB Islamic Bank Ltd
Eman Tabet	Research Associate	RFI Foundation
Abdelilah Talbioui	Head of Risk	Qatar Islamic Bank
Ikbal Taredia	Advisor to the CEO and Acting Director Capital Markets	ICD
Muhammad Umair Husain	Senior Investment Specialist	IsDB
Muhammad Usman Saleem	Manager procedures and process Implementation	Silkbank Limited pvt Pakistan
Shah Fahad Yousufzai	Regional Director MENA	Veefin Solutions ltd
Olatunji Yusuf	Senior Environmental Specialist	IsDB

Unlocking Islamic Climate Finance

This report analyzes how Islamic finance can be scaled up to help build urgently-needed climate-resilient infrastructure in the Asia and Pacific region, and ensure its post-COVID-19 recovery is green, sustainable, and inclusive. It outlines how greening Islamic capital markets and social finance, mobilizing project finance for infrastructure and boosting financial inclusion, can play a key role in funding the climate agenda. It details the 14 ADB developing member countries with majority Muslim populations, assesses the growth of the nearly $3 trillion global Islamic finance market, and explores how its faith-based principles support the transition to a green agenda.

About the Asian Development Bank

ADB is committed to achieving a prosperous, inclusive, resilient, and sustainable Asia and the Pacific, while sustaining its efforts to eradicate extreme poverty. Established in 1966, it is owned by 68 members —49 from the region. Its main instruments for helping its developing member countries are policy dialogue, loans, equity investments, guarantees, grants, and technical assistance.

About the Islamic Development Bank

The Islamic Development Bank (IsDB) is a multilateral development bank (MDB) working to improve the social and economic development of its member countries and Muslim communities around the world to deliver impact at scale. IsDB supports its member countries to meet their climate and sustainable development goals and targets through economic and social infrastructure investments, institutional strengthening, capacity building, partnership, and leveraging its resource-mobilization capabilities with other private, national, bilateral and multilateral development partners. IsDB is the world's largest public Islamic finance institution and the largest south-south MDB.

ADB **IsDB** البنك الإسلامي للتنمية
Islamic Development Bank

ASIAN DEVELOPMENT BANK
6 ADB Avenue, Mandaluyong City
1550 Metro Manila. Philippines
www.adb.org

www.ingramcontent.com/pod-product-compliance
Lightning Source LLC
Chambersburg PA
CBHW050051220326
41599CB00045B/7374